Restoring The Future

First Lesson Sermons
For Lent/Easter

Cycle A

Robert J. Elder

CSS Publishing Company, Inc., Lima, Ohio

Copyright © 2001 by
CSS Publishing Company, Inc.
Lima, Ohio

Scripture quotations are from the *New Revised Standard Version of the Bible*, copyright 1989 by the Division of Christian Education of the National Council of the Churches of Christ in the USA. Used by permission.

Library of Congress Cataloging-in-Publication Data

Elder, Robert J.
    Restoring the future : first lesson sermons for Lent/Easter, cycle A / Robert J. Elder.
      p. cm.
    ISBN 0-7880-1818-3 (alk. paper)
    1. Lenten sermons. 2. Holy-Week sermons. 3. Easter—Sermons. 4. Eastertide—Sermons. 5. Bible. O.T. Epistles—Sermons. 6. Bible. N.T. Acts—Sermons. 7. Sermons, American—21st century. I. Title.
BV4277 .E43 2001
252'.62—dc21
                                    2001025077
                                          CIP

For more information about CSS Publishing Company resources, visit our website at www.csspub.com.

ISBN 0-7880-1818-3   PRINTED IN U.S.A.

To the faithful
gathering of saints
at First Presbyterian Church,
Salem, Oregon, U.S.A.

Table Of Contents

Foreword

Too often preachers who use the lectionary simply default to the Gospel Lessons. Given the choice of a passage from the Gospels over against something from the Old Testament, Acts, or the Epistles, we quickly narrow the choice to one. After all, the Gospels are more familiar to us and to our congregations, the preaching resources for the Gospels are more plentiful, and we say to ourselves, "People seem to expect to hear a sermon from Matthew, Mark, Luke, or John," especially during the profound seasons like Lent and Easter.

However, to overlook the rest of the lectionary can severely diminish the possibilities, not only for pulpit creativity, but also for engaging and expanding the faithful imagination of the hearers. In this fine volume of sermons for Lent and Easter, Robert J. Elder, an accomplished Presbyterian pastor and preacher who lives in Salem, Oregon, challenges us to a deeper Easter faith, and he does so by opening up unexpected treasures from the First Lessons of the lectionary rather than the Gospel Lessons: passages from Genesis, Exodus, Samuel, the prophets, and the book of Acts.

Drawing upon thoughtfully mined biblical insights and his alert attention to contemporary culture, Rob Elder has crafted these sermons, and they not only disclose some unexpected angles of vision on Lent and Easter, they also can serve as models for preaching on neglected and overlooked texts.

A friend of mine recently went on a long-anticipated vacation with her husband to the Grand Canyon. They had collected guidebooks and articles from travel magazines on the Grand Canyon, and they had a file of photographs of the canyon at sunrise and sunset, in summer and winter. When my friend returned from her trip, she was full of excited memories, not only of the Grand Canyon, but also of some out-of-the-way sights they had stumbled on:

a small colony of native artists painting desert landscapes, a ghost town, a breathtakingly beautiful bend in a small stream where they had paused for a riverside picnic. "We expected to enjoy seeing the Grand Canyon," she said, "and we did. But it was what we didn't expect to see that delighted us the most."

So it is with these sermons. These are not the usual texts and these are not the expected words for the seasons of Lent and Easter, but it is sometimes what we do not expect to see and hear that delights us the most.

Thomas G. Long
Candler School of Theology
Emory University
Atlanta, Georgia

What Are They
Saying About Us?

Why should it be said among the peoples, "Where is their God?"

Where is your God? It may sound like a silly sort of statement, I suppose, but in some ways it is the deepest of theological questions. In childhood — and perhaps even in our adulthood — we may have thought casually about God living physically up in the sky, up in a heaven that is behind the clouds, apart from the earth. Silly as such notions may seem to us when we think about them, they are no sillier than the declarations made by early cosmonauts from the former Soviet Union who declared that since they saw no evidence of God or heaven when they went into space, atheism had been proven to be true.

Perhaps you have seen the recent ad on television which had a beautiful young female angel on a cloud, going to a celestial refrigerator to get a snack, which she then does not get around to sharing with her canine angel friend. Or the automobile dealer who ran a series of ads in which those who came to the gates of heaven having purchased their cars at competing dealerships were dropped suddenly through a trap door in the clouds to a fiery place below. Or the cartoon series on prime time network television called *God, the Devil, and Bob*. Or Woody Allen's famous line, "If only God would give me some clear sign! Like making a large deposit in my name at a Swiss bank." This is all the stuff of innumerable *New Yorker* cartoons and Peter-at-the-Pearly-Gates jokes. Is that the sort of place where we really believe God hangs out? Probably not, not in our more serious moments of contemplation.

Then where *is* your God? George Bernard Shaw once said, "Beware the man whose God is in the skies." So, if not among the cushy, heavenly cumulonimbus clouds, where then? What is the evidence that God is near, that God cares, that God keeps track of the doings on this earth? It's not a casual question. It is perhaps one of the most persistent of religious inquiries.

When Jesus hung on the cross, suspended on beams of wood, suspended between thieves, suspended between heaven and earth, the people mocked him, "He saved others," they said, "let him save himself if he is the Messiah of God" (Luke 23:35). "He trusts in God; let God deliver him now, if he wants to" (Matthew 27:43). Jesus himself cried out, "My God, my God! Why have you forsaken me?" (Matthew 27:46).

If that is not asking where God is, then I don't know a question when I hear one. The fact that Jesus could be brought to ask it gives us confidence in our own asking.

The prophets had an answer for such persistent questions. It was not to inquire into God's existence or whether people should believe there is a God, as if our believing or not believing makes any difference in the reality of God's existence. Seeking to confirm that the location of God was among them, they persistently inquired into the lives of God's chosen people, whether they were living in such a way that they would reflect rather than obscure the sense of the presence of God amid his people. The place God means to be is with God's people, but what is the evidence that God is there? The prophet asked, "Why should it be said among the peoples, 'Where is their God?'" and this is what he was getting at. If God is truly among us, if the place where God likes to hang his hat is, as Jesus said, near to us, (Luke 21:31), then our lives ought to demonstrate the reality of that.

In short, the Old Testament prophets, like Joel, believed it was necessary to live our faith, to make our living a constant reflection of the glory of God, so that those who see the believing community would not be given cause to wonder, "Where is their God?"

The lives of God's people would be the evidence that such a God was right there, right in their midst.

One of the ways that Joel knew the people could express their desire to be living reflections of the God they worshiped was to covenant together to repent of their shortcomings. And a powerful method by which they would express their repentance was through fasting — abstinence from certain foods — and a ceremonial rending of their clothing. But Joel recommended against a liturgical tearing of garments; he counseled them to rend their hearts instead, for only a heart that is cracked open and needy can receive the God who would enter in.

Today, when in some churches there is a ceremony marking worshipers' foreheads on Ash Wednesday with the ashes of the burned palms from the previous year's Palm Sunday, the intention is the same. It is to wear an outward reminder of an inward reality, an outward mark signifying a desire to rend one's heart through the course of the Lenten season so that God can enter in to save us.

Many Christian denominations haven't generally made such a big deal out of Ash Wednesday, though I know of many non-liturgical churches that have just such Ash Wednesday observances. Yet even many "high church" people fail to appear for services on Ash Wednesday. What is it about such an idea that most gives folks pause? Likely it is the public nature of it. We are reticent about being marked with ashes, and leaving them there the rest of the day for all to see. We are more often schooled in a privatized sort of religion, one we keep pretty much to ourselves unless we are in the company of people with whom we feel very safe. We do not generally wear our faith on our sleeves. We are the most likely people in Christendom to think of our faith as an individual matter, best left up to our own sense of God's presence with us. So among many of us there is often little chance of sporting ash-streaked foreheads, and often just as little chance of thinking on the communitarian sort of faith that Joel and all the prophets encouraged among the people.

So, what would be signs by which the world could see the presence of God in our midst, like the evidence of a great wind which shows not the wind but its effect? It is a long-standing Lenten discipline to reflect on Joel's recommendations for people seeking to be faithful witnesses to the presence of God among us in the ways he mentions:

Return. Turning, or, more to the point, *re*-turning to the path on which God sets the people is the goal of repentance. When we begin to walk away from God, to live our lives as though God doesn't exist, or that if God does exist, God's interest in our day-to-day existence is far from obvious and therefore, we are free to go our own individual ways, that is when we are called to turn around, to return to the path of faith in God.

Fasting. Fasting is not much valued in our culture or even in our church. But fasting is a way of remembering, a way of setting aside something that is common and familiar to us, so that space in our lives will be created to receive a word from God which we may have been overlooking in our filled-up lives. Fasting is a way of self-emptying to make room for the presence of God which God longs to supply.

Weeping and mourning. Why would anyone *seek* to do these things? Surely only a fool would recommend them as a religious discipline. Doesn't God want us to be happy? Shouldn't our lives be filled with happiness? But wait. It was Jesus who said, in the Beatitudes from his Sermon on the Mount, "Blessed are those who mourn, for they will be comforted ... Blessed are those who hunger and thirst for righteousness, for they will be filled" (Matthew 5:4, 6). Any kind of filling first requires an emptying. Most of us spend a good deal of our time being filled, filled with things to do, concerns, activities, work, relationships, hurrying from this to that appointment. And when our lives are not filled with necessary things, we fill them with additional things — television, sports, hobbies — anything and everything, just so long as they are full.

As an alternative to all this self-fulfillment, Joel recommends hearts broken for real, cracked open, so as to have room to receive the love which God longs to pour in, if only we could make room. All this returning and repenting and rending to which the Lenten season calls us is part of the difficult task for believers to discern God's presence again, and then to make responses in life that are not only personal but social, economic, even political.

All this is for the purpose of creating within ourselves, and for the sake of the world that looks on, a sense of the real presence of God among the people.

Is this not what Jesus represents to us, who have been added to the tree of Jesse by adoption through the Christian church? Isn't the life and death of Jesus among us the evidence to which we point when we think about whether God is present among us? Is it not Jesus who promised to be among us when two or three are gathered in his name?

Joel asked the question, and not rhetorically: "Why should it be said among the peoples, 'Where is their God?' " Well, why should it? If we are God's people, truly God's people, then our lives are meant to be the evidence of God's life among us.

God went to the trouble of offering himself to us in Jesus, in the person of the Messiah, in order to be among us. When people know we are a church of Christ, gathered in this place, why should it be said among them as they see us coming and going in our busy church existence, "Where is their God?"

A Fear Of Falling

Three observations:

1. If newspaper accounts at the time were accurate, one of the reasons Donald Trump began having second thoughts about his marriage — and the meaning of his life in general — can be traced to the accidental deaths of two of his close associates. The most profound way he could find to describe his reaction sounded typically *Trumpian*. He said that he could not understand the meaning behind the loss of two people "of such quality."

2. A heroic account of the work of a Protestant pastor — who conspired to hide and transport Jews in German-occupied France during World War II — opens with the story of the death of his mother.[1] When he was a boy, his family was in an automobile accident in which his mother was killed. That proved to be a turning point in his life. The contemplation of his mother's lifeless body there on the road and his father's reckless driving that had killed her led him to affirm that human life is infinitely precious, whether it was the life of the Jews who were fleeing the Nazis, or the lives of the Nazis themselves.

3. One bright morning along between the ages of 35 to fifty, many people look at themselves in the mirror and are struck by the dawning realization that they are no longer what our society calls "young people." They begin to discover that the models on television, the actors that get the best roles, and the folks who pose with products in magazines are increasingly selected from people younger than themselves. Professional football, baseball, and basketball players their own age are either relegated to the sidelines

or described as "aging veterans." Sure, there are likely to be comments from folks in their seventies and eighties about how they would love to be forty again, but the widespread use of the phrase, *mid-life crisis*, suggests that there is a special developmental task for those of us in this mid-life period of life which must be accomplished if we are ever to reach a well-adjusted viewpoint at sixty, seventy, or eighty. At age forty we have reached a time in which the end is in sight, when — statistically speaking — there is more time spent than remaining, and that the time which remains will include the subtle and not-so-subtle deterioration of physical abilities, accompanied by the increasing awareness of aches, pains, and assorted medical problems that now won't just go away.

What do these three random observations have in common? Just this: the awareness — unique among all animals to the human animal — that we are mortal. Like the other animals, our bodies are not designed to last forever. Unlike other animals, we know in advance that this is so. Just because this has always been so does not make each generation's accommodation to it any easier. Why is this pertinent to us on a Sunday morning? Because this is precisely what our readings from Genesis can help us to understand.

In his best-selling book, *When Bad Things Happen To Good People* (Schocken Books, 1989), Rabbi Harold Kushner correctly observed that people do not fear death itself as much as we fear what death might mean. Does the fact that I will die one day mean that my life has been meaningless? Does it mean that all the good things of life — the love we have experienced, the care that we have shared with others, the accomplishments we have managed to leave behind — are erased by our parting? Will my death be a time in which I am abandoned by those who once loved me, and all my life's work will be seen as futile?

Our story in Genesis declared that God took dust from the earth, blew into it the mysterious and still little-understood breath of life, and God's relationship with humanity was underway. Later, after the disobedience in the garden (where God's warning turned out not to be that they would die if they ate the forbidden fruit so much as that they would *know* they would die), the nineteenth verse of the third chapter says that from that point on, people would have to toil their existence out of the very dust to which they would ultimately return. Our own toil in the earth would serve as a daily reminder of our mortality. Humanity not only has to live with the fact that death ends our lives, but we have to live with the knowledge of that fact as well.

I have a friend who has a beautiful golden retriever at home. One day he will die and his master will weep. But the dog doesn't know that, and is not confronted with daily reminders of his impending mortality. He eats, sleeps, and launches himself into gravity-defying leaps when he thinks he is going to have a ride in the car. His life is generally serene. His death is no source of anxiety for him today.

Not so with us. The story in Genesis proclaims that our daily toil will remind us that we will die, in echoes that are as unavoidable for billionaire entrepreneurs and French pastors as for 48-year-old people in mourning for their vanishing youth. There shall be no exception to this rule. Its reminders will shadow us until the shadow one day claims us. That is the curse laid upon Adam and Eve in eating of the tree of knowledge of good and evil, and whether we believe this is a good explanation of its origin or not, it is a fact of our lives to this very minute, as up-to-date as the morning newspaper. Death always makes the news. It always has. It always will.

Where does that leave us? Paul believed death was the result of sin, so that universal human mortality was the proof of our universal sin (Romans 5:12-19). The number one sin throughout the Bible is the sin of idolatry, generally setting ourselves up as little gods in the rightful place of our Creator God. When the serpent promised that they would become like God, he didn't mention that it meant knowing something it would have been better to have let God keep to himself. Adam and Eve stand for all of disobedient humanity, but Paul suggested a new era has begun, that in view of the resurrection of Jesus, there is a new possibility open to humanity in addition to the necessity of sin and death: it is grace and life.

Clearly, this passage from Genesis shows that the biblical idea of sin goes well beyond a concern with little transgressions we may have committed on this or that occasion. The more fundamental problem for humanity, which the story of Adam and Eve shows to be a problem originating deep in the mists of human prehistory, is a rebellion against God. Further, it is a rebellion which — despite our best efforts — we are powerless to overcome. Try as we might, we make ourselves the measure of this world and the good God who created it, rather than letting our God be the measure of us, God's creatures. We are "incurably prone to the idolatry of regarding ourselves rather than God as the final hope of our redemption."[2]

If Jesus had not shared this curse of death with us, then he could not have been truly human. If he had not contemplated with dread the prospect of his own death, he would have been only a pretender to community with us. But the entirety of his life and ministry makes clear the fact that he placed his whole trust and confidence in his heavenly Father. Paul declared that because of that unique sinless quality, Jesus has become the new Adam, creating the possibility for life where before there was only the possibility for death. Jesus has led us from the gates outside the Garden of Eden through the Garden of Gethsemane, to the gates of heaven. God raised Jesus from the dead, and his example of a new humanity makes possible an altogether new contemplation of the finality of our existence. Lives void of any other meaning may now be filled with the meaning that Jesus' life gives us.

We have entered Lent this week, but it is important that as we enter this season, we not lose sight of Easter and the hope of eternity which Easter provides. Our dread of death is taken up in God's ringing affirmation of life in Christ. Praise be to God whose victory is ours in Jesus Christ!

---

1. Philip Hallie, *Lest Innocent Blood Be Shed* (Harper & Row, 1979), p. 53.

2. Paul Achtemeier, *Romans*, Interpretation Commentary Series (Louisville: John Knox Press, 1985), p. 101.

Dependable Faith

Drop the Gordita! Have you seen the Taco Bell ad with the window washer who doesn't want to lose his lunch? He hangs between heaven and earth by a thread, as if it is difficult to make up his mind whether to hold on to his taco, or drop it in order to cling to the rope offered by those who would save him.

I once read about a man washing windows outside a large office building.[1] When he reached the fifteenth floor, he slipped on the scaffolding that supported him on the side of the building, and just managed to catch a tenuous hold on a line that dangled below the scaffold. He hung there suspended, his grip growing increasingly weak, when someone inside the building spotted him, broke a window, and grabbed hold of him until help arrived. Now it could be said that at the moment of his rescue, the window washer had a choice to make. He could either have caught the hand of his rescuer, or he could as easily have chosen to plummet to his death on the street below. Not surprisingly, he chose the gift of rescue when it was offered.

One of the common interpretations of God's call to Abraham to travel to a far country suggests that Abraham's response involved a brave and costly leaving behind of all that was familiar, setting out on a journey to some place unfamiliar, waving a choked-up farewell to kith and kin in order to set out on a noble sojourn, a quest. This view just misses the point by a whisker, coming close enough to be a tempting distraction from what is really the more central issue. It is like focusing on the window washer's choice to grab the hand that was offered, rather than on the unexpected and gracious quality of the gift of rescue that came quite apart from the window washer's ability to choose or not choose. So we frequently hear calls to leave familiar things behind and take on risks, taking up brave quests, based on this reading from Genesis, focusing on what we might do to be brave, risk-taking people, when in reality Abraham was just as much at the end of his rope as the window washer. His only real choices were between oblivion and God's command to set out for a new land. If we do not find our responses to God coming in just such neediness as that of the window washer, we will never really fathom the meaning of the story of Abraham and what it means for our faith.

Abraham was called to depart from country, kindred, even his father's house to an unspecified land which God would show him. It sounds for all the world like the heart-rending pictures of late nineteenth century immigrants embarking from European ports to travel to unknown and much misunderstood America, faces in the crowd on Ellis Island in New York harbor, frightened, wondering what their new lives had in store for them. It is a natural way to look at Abraham's call, but not entirely on the mark unless we recall that for most of those immigrants — as for the window washer — their choice was one made in desperation, as a last hope for their lives.

To begin with, consider the fact that Abraham was a nomad. His people were wandering shepherds. One rocky hillside looks pretty much like another when one spends most of the time looking for good country on which to graze livestock. They weren't really settled people at all. They didn't have "a country" in the sense that we do. Consider also that Abraham's father, Terah, had already died — as reported in Genesis 11:32, the verse immediately preceding the beginning of our Genesis passage. That makes a command to leave the patriarchal homestead appear a little less traumatic, doesn't it? What was left there to exercise a hold on Abraham?

Consider also that in the verses just preceding our passage, Abraham's father had moved the family from a country called Ur to one called Haran, even though he had been intending to get to the land called Canaan — so their settlement in Haran was really temporary to begin with. And consider the fact that Abraham was 75 when he answered God's call to go to a new country. Hardly a brave youth responding to the appeal of adventure in a new country! More like a tired old fellow with not many more steps left until the one that would lead to the same place where his father now rested. And finally — perhaps most importantly — consider the fact that just before our morning passage, Genesis reported, rather matter-of-factly, that Abraham's wife, Sarah, was "barren; she had no child" (Genesis 11:30).

Exactly what was Abraham leaving behind when he answered God's call to travel to a new country? A dead father, in a land to which he had developed no great attachment, and no children, no heirs. God had managed to single out a dead-end family living on the edge of oblivion to offer to them a call to go to a new country, a new start. Sarah's barrenness was perhaps the most visible reminder of what was by then an obvious human dead-end. Here was a family destined for extinction. Like a window washer with a slipping grip and a life flashing before his eyes, humanly speaking there was no self-generating future, no possibility, no hope. It was just such a family, empty of hope, which God singled out for a call, not some brave, responsive, forward-thinking hero, but a dusty, dead-end, wretched family. When Paul once wrote in Romans 4 that Abraham had nothing to boast about, it was this that he meant, at least in part. Abraham's response to God's call reflects no particular credit on Abraham. What other choice did he have, but to sit down and die? The window washer doesn't deserve a lot of credit for his rescue, except for having had the good sense to have grabbed the rescuing hand when it was offered.

God provided for Abraham not only the choice to follow the path of faith which leads to life, but did so in circumstances that made this particular gift glitter all the brighter like a sunny, sandy island of promise standing in a dark and treacherous sea of hopelessness.

And there is more. The hand that reached out to rescue the window washer reached out for more than the rescue of just one person. Were the rescue not offered, had the window washer fallen and died, the repercussions would have extended to the company that had employed him, the family that had loved him, the wife and children — if he had any— that would now have to learn to live without him, and beyond.

The rescue of this Abraham who had no living father and no hope of a son salvaged more than a family of nomadic shepherds in ancient Palestine. God promised this heirless old man not only that he would have a son, but more, that he would become father of a great nation, and even more, that he would be a name that would serve as a blessing to every family on earth. That's a pretty good stretch in just four verses — from childless vagabond to a blessing for humanity!

In reverse order from the list of dead-end things he was to leave behind — country, kindred, father's house — Abraham was to bear a promise of untold proportions to an ever-broadening circle: a blessed name, a blessed nation, a blessing for the whole human family. The proportions of that gift are still being worked out in the human family to this day.

Saint Paul — in his theological genius — saw this more clearly perhaps than anyone before or since. Just when humanity had realized in one tragic event after another — disobedience in the garden, murder of Abel by his brother Cain, the Great Flood, the confusion at the tower of Babel — that it had no power to invent a future, a future was given through a man who personally showed utterly no signs of promise.

Humanity, barren of potential of its own providing, is precisely the sort of ground where God speaks the word of Good News. Dead ends are the places where God begins to make highways of hope. From the story of Abraham we can see that God clearly does not depend on some human potential residing in the ones needing rescue. God's work is always a sort of resurrection. Paul says as much: God "... gives life to the dead and calls into existence the things that do not exist" (Romans 4:17).

God's purpose hinges only on the willingness of the dying one to grasp the hand that rescues it. The gift of God depends on our willingness to receive it, which means finally acknowledging that the true initiative to choose life is held by someone other than ourselves. This sets itself in especially startling contrast with much of the assumptive world of modern times which begins with the presumption that there is only us. All the good gifts that humanity might crave are dependent on the acknowledgement that God has something in mind for us beyond our own conceiving.

Now, in every time there have been — as there are in our time — people who thought it was still possible to gain salvation the old fashioned way, by earning it. These were the folks we meet every day, who tell us that they are relatively certain that they will make it to heaven because they have led a pretty good life and that God surely wouldn't deny heaven to people who are pretty good. Abraham's own life demonstrates that any works — good or otherwise — which are performed with a view to justification are destined to fall short and to belittle the gift of God. God's relationship with Abraham was not based on his leading a pretty good life — we really have no idea what sort of life he led up to age 75 — but on his neediness and his response to the rescuing love of God. Emptied of self, he was willing to be filled with the promise of God. Void of any rightful claims on God, he was open to a gift when it came his way.

If we are not quite like Abraham — that is, if we have not reached a dead end, we have plenty to live for — we might not find it easy to accept the idea of God's purpose for our lives and our world as a gift which we don't deserve. It seems impossible. We subscribe to the human tendency to try to earn God's favor. It is just when we are in such a state of mind — especially if we're failing at it — that it is so helpful to reflect on the likes of Abraham. God's gift — made available to a dead-end straggler like Abraham — will surely be made available to us. All we have to do is close our fingers around that rescuing hand.

And of course, we are doubly blessed, because we know of God's care not as a misty promise of land and descendants, but as the saving love expressed in a savior who is Jesus, who came to us — like God's promise came to Abraham — quite apart from our deserving, quite in spite of our non-deserving. It is ultimately this hand which reaches out to save us. This hand, crucified, nail-pierced, and beckoning to us, is extended on this day and forever. Oh, won't you grasp it? Won't you rescue not only yourself but all those who come after and may bless themselves by your name because of the one who has made himself a blessing for you? I pray that we will.

_____

1. William Jones, *The Upper Room*, March 2, 1974.

Identity Crisis

Recently, in a weekly Bible study, the group poured over this Exodus passage, and someone remarked, "I am impressed by how contemporary this sounds." The Exodus story? *Contemporary?* Generally we think of it as anything *but* contemporary! Near the dawn of recorded human history a band of primitive Middle Eastern Bedouins, having fled from Egypt, now makes its way on foot through the savage desert wilderness. The threat of death and disease from the ever present dangers lingers over them like a cloud; they have no sense of scientific certainty, no sense of geography; they are not even sure where they are going or why. Contemporary? Is your life like that? Is mine?

Backed up against the Red Sea and fearing for their lives, the Hebrews had complained bitterly to Moses about their safety — but they were rescued; later, worried over the long desert trek ahead of them and fearful that their provisions might not prove to be enough, they moaned and accused Moses again — yet they were fed by the manna; later yet, now fretting over their water supply, they accused Moses of trying to kill them by dehydration — and again they received the fulfillment of their needs; later yet, in a passage from Numbers 11, if you're interested in cataloging the complaints of the Israelites, you will find them even complaining over the menu because, it seems, their diet of manna and quail and water had become boring. When things were going badly or when things were going well, the one constant seemed to be their complaining.

25

Captains of ocean-going ships tell lots of interesting stories, but one I've heard which seems so appropriate to this Exodus account comes from cruise ship captains. Most unseasoned travelers will say they dread a storm at sea more than anything. But often, after seven glorious sunsets, seven days of shuffleboard on the lower deck, seven days of swimming in the pool on the upper deck, seven days of sumptuous feasts at every meal and often between meals, and seven nights of refreshments and beautiful music and dancing, some passenger is bound to turn to the captain at some point in the voyage and ask hopefully, "Do you think we'll have a storm?" Satisfaction with what we have received just doesn't seem to be part of the human capacity, does it? And that is as contemporary as the last time we complained about the limited choices on a restaurant menu.

The continual murmuring and complaining of the Hebrews in their desert wandering had only partly to do with real human needs. If we look at their murmuring against Moses concerning water, at first glance it sounds like a pretty legitimate complaint. "Hey, Moses! What are you thinking about? Didn't you know that people have been known to get thirsty in the desert? Did you choreograph this grand escape but forget to make plans for water for the thousands of us?"

On the surface of things, it sounds legitimate enough. Just ask any of the troops who stood on the sun-bleached sand of the Saudi Arabian desert whether they thought it was important for their commanders to have made plans concerning water supplies. If there were no such plans you can bet they would be complaining in voices just as loud and just as anxious as the ancient Israelites. So that is at least one way this story sounds contemporary. But there may be more.

I am struck especially in realizing that Moses found their complaint went far beyond a request for water. They said, "Give us water to drink," and he responded, saying, "Why do you find fault with me? Why do you put the Lord to the test?" Then he turned to God and said, "They are almost ready to stone me!" Now, what did he hear that I didn't hear? They are thirsty, they are anxious about it, they ask him to provide water since he seems to be in charge of this enterprise, but here is where Moses senses a danger quite apart from a physical need for water. It is a danger that has to do with perception, with attitude, with the deeper places in our souls which may surface as nothing more than complaining, but which reveal so much more about us. Moses knows better than anyone there that since he first set his eyes on the burning bush in the wilderness around Midian that he is definitely *not* in charge. When they find the accommodations to be less than they require, their conflict is not with Moses, it is with the author of this whole undertaking and that is God, and that is why Moses wants to know why they insist on putting God to the test, why in their request for water there lingers a doubt that in God's own way, provision has been made for them.

He was right on target. "Why did you bring us up out of Egypt, to kill us and our children and our cattle with thirst?" They have moved from requesting water to doubting their election by God, questioning the very nature of their salvation. Why did you bring us up, Moses? They are saying, in effect, there is no God, there is only Moses, and if we had to choose a king to rule us and give us food and water, we'd just as soon have Pharaoh who has much more experience with this sort of thing anyway.

Whining and complaining against a world where we have already pretty much decided to live as though God wasn't present anyway, where we are more or less left to our own devices, our own craftiness, where the very last thing we consider in making our daily decisions about which clothes to wear, what to shop for at the grocery store, what arrangements to make for the weekend, what car to buy, as though God had no interest or care concerning those day-to-day plans — yes, this sounds more and more contemporary to me all the time. These weren't stupid people who failed to see God's obvious presence among them. Rather, God's presence seemed anything but obvious to them, as often the presence of God is anything but obvious to us in the ordinary course of our days. When the passage closes with the naming of that watering place with the remembrance, "Is the Lord among us or not?" it could be the very contemporary cry of modern people. Honestly now, in what ways is it obvious to you and to me from day to day that God is an ever-present reality?

These people were in the midst of an identity crisis. The only thing that made them a people rather than a mob was their calling from God. Apart from that, they were likely just to become a mob, and act like one, as Moses' fear of being stoned makes evident. Any time they began to lose sight of the One who had called them to be his people, they simultaneously forgot who they were. It can happen to us. That is why so often churches cease being places where the gospel is preached and where the people strive to align their lives to that gospel, and instead become sort of shadow social service agencies or cozy fellowship clubs or fashion shows, anything but a called people who know whether the Lord is among them or not. Yes, this is sounding more contemporary to me all the time.

The Psalmist described God as "the rock of our salvation," and there is little doubt that this is the Bible story he had in mind, this story of water from a rock. But we so seldom live as though God were truly the rock of salvation — the very foundation on which our lives are built. More often we live by our wits and think of God as a bearded, distant, disinvolved old man from childhood stories we once knew.

Jesus called Peter, called all of the disciples, really, the rock on which his church would be built. Why? Because they were exceptionally daring or wily or crafty? Because they knew how to organize thousands, develop snappy new initiatives? No, rather because they had a glimmer of the source of their new life, the nature of the One who was prepared to save them from living as though their own craftiness was all there was in the world that they could rely on.

As individuals, or even as a group, apart from their confession of Jesus as Messiah, they would have no identity. The church is not created, formed, introduced by individuals on their own authority, initiative, insight. The leaders of the first or any church — this one included — are not called to be reliable anywhere nearly as much as we are called to be reliant, reliant on a power not our own, on a power which has called us to be God's special people, has set us apart, not made us more like the rest of the world, but different, distinct, a community of witness to the world, what Paul calls "a colony of heaven." The church is not the result of a free undertaking of people who have gathered together to decide which doctrines and confessions best suit our needs and seem most appropriate to us. Karl Barth — theological veteran of the World War II years in Europe — said we should have the right and the duty to appeal to the grace of God to be blessed outside of such a church, a church made by our own hands, our own wits.

The church — like the people of Israel — has nothing to do with human initiative, human insight, human empowerment, even self-generated human liberation, and everything to do with God's decision and act of self-revelation, whether at a watering rock at Horeb, or before Peter and the disciples in the form of Jesus of Nazareth. The decision, the initiative, as it turns out, is entirely God's.

Which is how it is with what we think and know of ourselves once we have made the heart-felt confession that Jesus is Lord. It is not even an act for which we can entirely make account in and of ourselves. Even our confession is part of God's graciousness. We know who we are, not because of self-esteem or self-motivation, but because God has declared in Christ for us just who and what we might become. We might become children of God.

The search for identity has been the cry of our age. Going out to find ourselves was the fascination of my generation, and to a large degree, still is. The result of such inward searches is often that we discover there is less of us than we had wished there would be. Reliance upon our individual resources is seldom a reliance upon something entirely dependable.

Not long ago, a friend of mine sat in a church staff meeting, and as he did, he realized he was gathered with incredibly gifted people the congregation had asked to come and help make their church into a witnessing community. And because theirs was a church full of incredible gifts and abilities and energy, naturally they had called staff members who mirrored a lot of what they were. It was an amazingly competent and able staff of people whose source of energy sometimes seemed boundless. They were so —

well, *reliable*. And because they are a reliable group, folks that one can count on almost as surely as we can count on the sunrise, it occurred to him that perhaps even reliability can sometimes be an idol, can give us a false sense of self-sufficiency. And as he sought to find words for a prayer with the staff that day, it occurred to him to ask God to make them ever more *reliant*. With this group, reliable takes care of itself. Being reliant on the power that called us to be a people, that is the self-emptied style of living that often escapes us.

If we would build the kingdom, we must be reliant even more than we are reliable. We must be made to see every day who it is that calls and sustains us. In the end, an identity crisis for a people boils down to knowing whose we are more than who we are. We are children of God, servants of the God of Israel, who calls us to be his own. May God make us equal to that calling.

The Office Of The King
Was Not Vacant

Not all the water in the rough rude sea
Can wash the balm from an anointed king.
                                        — Richard II, William Shakespeare

How long will you grieve over Saul? I have rejected
him from being king over Israel. Fill your horn with
oil and set out.

When we drop into the scriptures, as we tend to do on Sunday mornings, visiting this and then that spot in various books of the Bible, what tends to get lost is the long-term flow of the larger narrative, the place in the whole long story of the kings of Israel where this particular portion of the story takes place, for instance. If we read over just the verses that have been chosen for today's service, we might be left with the impression that by the time we reach verse 14, the rule of King Saul is at an end, that David has become ascendant. While this may have been true in the mind of God at the moment of David's anointing, it is going to take fifteen more chapters for the full impact of the news to trickle all the way up to Saul. Saul may have lost favor with God, but no human being much wants to be the bearer of *that* message to a sitting king.

Samuel was one of the great prophets of Israel. It had been Samuel whom God chose to seek and anoint Israel's first king, and as he scanned through the tribes he had chosen Saul, who stood "head and shoulders" above everyone else (1 Samuel 9:2; 10:23). Judging by his impressive external appearance, which is

31

likely the way any warrior king would most frequently be judged, Saul seemed to be more than qualified, seemed destined to succeed. But he had not succeeded, not by God's measure at any rate. He turned out to be like so many human leaders, more interested in erecting monuments to himself than in seeing to the welfare of the people. By the time we reach the portion of the story we share today, his life has ground to a virtual halt with aberrant behavior that suggests madness, a blindness to any vision of God's purpose for this chosen people. He was clinging to power for the sake of power alone. So Samuel was called upon to seek and anoint a new king, even though the office of the sitting king was not yet vacant. This is not something that one would normally do, anoint a new king when the current king is still occupying the throne. Sitting kings tend to take a dim view of such things. Being a prophet in such circumstances is dangerous work; it should merit battlefield pay.

In the chapters that follow this, David will meet up with Goliath and defeat him on the field of battle. And instead of receiving the gratitude of the king, he will look up just in time to dodge a spear which the king will have chucked at him. He will marry Saul's daughter Michal, a loveless, arranged marriage which Saul will finagle in order to improvise a way that David might be killed by the Philistines as he attempts to secure a wedding prize for his future father-in-law. Eventually, David will be forced to flee Saul's royal court and begin to live the life of an outlaw and fugitive. He will have to make alliance with enemies of Saul, go into the service of the king of Gath, even fight alongside the hated Philistines in order to stay alive. Twice David will find himself in a position to kill the sleeping king, but twice he won't do it, using the evidence of his refusal to harm Saul as testimony to his fealty to a king who no longer deserves his loyalty. Finally, in chapter 31, beleaguered and outnumbered, Saul will fall on his own sword in battle.

So the anointing of Jesse's youngest and least-likely son — this is only the beginning of the troubles for David, the boy who would be king, for the office of king was not vacant, not by a long shot. And we all know how gladly kings receive the news that their replacement is on the way. Recall how delighted Herod was to hear from the Magi about a king to be born in Bethlehem.

Let's take a look at the boy David, whom God favored above his seven older brothers. The first thing we need to note is that youngest birth-order children love stories like this account of David. The youngest, weakest, the one seemingly so unlikely to be chosen for anything special, the antithesis of the dramatically imposing Saul, the one whose father almost forgot he had him — this is the very one God has in mind to be the greatest king Israel has ever known, the one next to whom all other kings before or since have been measured, the one from whose line Jesus came.

There is some good news in this that we might not have expected. Beholden as we are to the culture of entertainment that celebrates exclusively the rich, the powerful, the beautiful people, the story of humble David — smallest of eight brothers, citizen of the smallest clan in Israel, the one whose father almost forgot him out standing up to his ankles in sheep droppings in the field behind the house — this story reminds us that the hero God chooses is often the unfinished one, the unlikely one, the one that only after he or she has succeeded beyond anyone's wildest imaginings do we find ourselves saying, "Of *course*, it had to be him; it couldn't have been anyone else *but* her." God sometimes goes in search of the least likely candidate to be God's champion, and that candidate will sometimes be you, even when you feel least up to the task, perhaps especially then. It will be you even though the office of king is not yet vacant. Never mind that, trust the promise of God, it carries all the strength needed. Why is this, do you suppose? One line tells all. "For the Lord does not see as human beings see; they look on outward appearance, but the Lord looks on the heart." This so reminds me of Antoine Saint Exupery's *Little Prince*, where we read, "And now here is my secret, a very simple secret: It is only with the heart that one can see rightly; what is essential is invisible to the eye."

Samuel had tried going by outward appearance once before and it didn't work out for him. This time, God was in search of a leader who had the insides for the job. That is why this is good

33

news for any of us who have cherished even a small burning ember of desire to do something significant for the Lord. That tiny, unformed willingness can be put to work even if we believe ourselves to be far from ready. Recall that the people who remembered and passed this story down were more like David than Saul. The people Israel were small potatoes, marginalized, barely a footnote in the historical records of kingdoms and empires except for their own record in the Bible. The story was remembered by people who often need to recall from time to time that even among the marginalized, the beside-the-point people, there is undiscovered capacity for greatness.

Here is the way one pastor spoke about the opening line of our passage: " 'Now the Lord said to Samuel, "How long will you grieve over Saul?" ' And while it's unusual for a story to start that way, it's also true that the question's a natural. Whenever there is a collapse of leadership ... that vacuum is the arena of grief; grief over what might have been and won't be yet until new leadership emerges. So it's interesting that the Lord doesn't say: don't grieve. The question is *how long*? ... Because grief does prevent us from entering the future, and as long as we live in the kingdom of what might have been, we aren't really ready to move forward."[1]

Who is the king? What place does a king have in the life of a people who believe that God is the ruler of the universe, the true King of the people? In Israel, there existed a continuing, dramatic tension between two major establishments: the religious authorities and the secular authorities. Samuel's prophetic office in Israel expressed God's reluctance to give the people the king they craved. The reason is the all-too-common human temptation to believe that human heroes are worthy of our worship, and the equally human temptation of our heroes to believe they are right. In some ways, our lives represent a series of overthrows of the kings who lay claim to the thrones of our hearts. It is an on-going process, never completed but always in progress.

We awake one day in our earliest childhood memory with our parents on the throne, seeming gods, yet they exist alongside the increasing awareness of our separateness from them. While they are still on the throne — the office of king in our lives not yet vacated by them — we begin the process of anointing ourselves rulers over our own lives. This contest for the throne generally comes to a head in adolescence, when, even though the king of self-awareness still sits on the throne, we anoint as rulers over us the tyrannical opinions and company of our peers. If we are here this morning through some means other than coercion, chances are good that at some point we also began to recognize another Pretender to the throne of our lives. But this one is gentle, not a tyrant. While parents, self, peers, and eventually career, family, relationships may all have found themselves struggling for the throne of our lives at one time or another — perhaps all at the same time — this Pretender to the throne does not join the fight in the usual way.

Others may claim a place as the rightful rulers in our lives because they are strongest, most beautiful, most influential, most popular. But this One, already anointed by the shedding of his blood on the cross, is not to be regarded by outward appearances, which could appear weak, even horrifying. This claimant to the throne is to be judged by his heart. And his heart, descended from the spacious heart of David himself, from the very throne of God, his heart is capacious enough to include all of us, to meet our secret, most fervent and unmet desire to have a truly benevolent ruler in our lives that cares for our well-being more than he cares for his own.

There are rejected kings aplenty who have competed for the right to rule over us. We may spend our whole lives honoring one or another of them, battling the new King, the rightful King, who is descended from the line of David; we may even crucify him in our attempt to deny him our throne. But that he will reign is a promise of God. All our fighting will not change the outcome, only our own suffering in it.

Even if the office of King is not vacant in your life, there is an Anointed One who claims the throne. But he will not take it by force. His reign is not like that. He awaits your acquiescence. Yet he will not rest until he makes his home on the throne of your heart.

---

1. George Chorba, "In The Kingdom Of Nobodies," unpublished manuscript.

Lent 5
Ezekiel 37:1-14

Life In The Old Bones Yet

Several years ago a psychologist conducted a survey in which he asked 3,000 people the question, "What are you living for?" He was not at all ready for the results. He discovered that ninety percent of his respondents were — as he put it — "simply putting up with the present while they waited for the future." We are all familiar with the feeling. We spend today thinking about what will happen tomorrow: young couples wait for their wedding day; children wait for Christmas; at 64 we wait for retirement; at 34 we wait for success.

I read once that such preoccupation with the future is like looking through binoculars at a dimly visible scene in the distance, while trampling on the exquisite flower garden at our feet. Perhaps it is true that we should not waste today by mortgaging the life we have been given here and now for some imagined future time of happiness.

When does life begin and when does it end? Or, perhaps more to the point, when are we really living, and when are we just marking time?

According to the United States Bureau of Statistics, there are approximately fifty million people in the country who cannot furnish legal proof that they were ever born. That's more than the number that watch late night television each night! But of that number, how many do you suppose are really living anyway, regardless what the Bureau of Statistics says? How many of us are really living? Probably the psychologist's survey would give us a

37

clue. No doubt many of us spend too much time putting up with the present while waiting for the future.

Different people would give different answers to questions about real living and when life begins and ends.

The professional athlete would say that life begins just after college and is over at age 35 or so, when most professional athletes are all washed up. Does it ever strike you as strange that athletes can talk of a whole professional career, and be speaking of a span of ten to fifteen years at the most?

The professional lawyer or physician would likely say that life begins at thirty or 35 (just about the time the athlete's career is ending), when his career really begins to get into full swing.

How do you suppose Arthur Rubenstein, the great pianist, would have answered the question, "When does real life begin?" Just before he died at age 95 he wrote, "I'm passionately involved in life: I love its changes, its colors, its movement. To be alive, to be able to see, to walk, to have houses, music, paintings ... it's all a miracle."

Real living seems to be a matter of individual perception, colored by circumstances and choices made as we go along.

If the television industry were to be taken as a guide for finding out about real life, the process of living would seem to involve a long, drawn-out battle with the inevitable, the inevitable being that it is in the nature of things for living creatures to die one day. Whether it is a washed-up 37-year-old basketball player, or a 95-year-old concert pianist, we are all headed in the same direction, but we all would like to put it off as long as possible. So as we watch television we discover we have creams to make us look younger, cars to make us look younger, razor blades to make us look younger. Practically everything we can buy is sold to us with the implicit promise that it is the youthful thing to do. Not too long ago I read about a California couple that was making huge sums of money with a new technique for healthful living. The main promise and selling point was that it would add years to your life and keep you younger looking longer through proper intake of vitamins and avoidance of fatty foods, coupled with vigorous exercise. As I looked at their advertisements, with examples of their regimen of strenuous exercise and a diet so carefully monitored that it would make a hospital dietitian nervous, I wondered if this is really living! Does real living simply mean making life last longer?

The preoccupation with the young and the hope for a long life masks the fear that all humanity shares, as we look over our shoulders, seeing that death stalks every one of us. If we were trying to understand the world and our part in it by looking at nature, we would have to say that it appears to be a world in which the main rule is: death overcomes life. Life may have its day, but death has the last word. For every living form known to us, death awaits.

Paul wrote to the Romans, "To set the mind on the flesh is death." If the whole purpose of life is wrapped up in putting off the inevitable, then life is a pretty pathetic thing, its possibility of beauty diminished with the passing of every moment, and certainly with the passing of every human being we know. We want to moan, with the writer of Ecclesiastes, "All is vanity."

A friend of mine remembers an eerie scene of hopelessness from a family trip to New Mexico one summer. He took part in a paleontology dig in the rugged desert country around the Presbyterian conference center at Ghost Ranch. At one location they discovered the fossilized remains of a dinosaur known as "Coelophysis." After unearthing a good portion of the skeleton, they learned that dozens of other similar animals had been found at the same location through the years. It must have been a watering hole in some long lost time, and on one day, or during one short period, a whole host of these animals perished on that very spot; no one knows by what cause. There they lay — skeletons intact — all these millions of years, until a bunch of amateur paleontologists happened along to dig them up. Life in the animal world seems capable of an end just as futile as life in the human world, only we have the dubious privilege of knowing ahead of time where we are bound.

There are two very human responses to the knowledge that we will all die one day. The *first* is to do what the psychologists have discovered that hundreds of us do: we avoid thinking about the inevitable by continually creating a future for ourselves. If today I have made plans for Thursday night, I believe that surely I will still be here on Thursday to see them through. So we live life, not today, but for what will happen tomorrow. If that seems to be a faulty way of seeing the world, looking through binoculars toward a future happiness while trampling the daisies at our feet, we might be tempted to favor a *second* response. That is to live for the moment. One song of the '60s, forgettable in almost every way, which nevertheless has a tendency to stick in the brain, had a refrain which went, "Sha, la, la, la, la, la, live for today,.../And don't worry 'bout tomorrow, hey, hey, hey." It seems to be an appropriate hymn for that time, when so many were caught up in living for the present moment: grasp the moment, go for all the gusto, you only go 'round once.

But both responses, human and understandable, are still part of what Paul saw as a prevalent attitude of his day: "To set the mind on the flesh is death."

Both the "present mortgaged to the future" and the "spend-thrift present" produce the same result: One day there will be — as there was on that dry desert floor in New Mexico — death and a valley of dry bones. We may even provide the skeletons for some future amateur paleontologist to ponder over thousands of years hence. Whether we are free spirits or cautious conservatives, "to set the mind on the flesh is death." Seeing life in this dimension alone sends us all in the direction of the valley of the shadow without a clue as to why it must be so.

But there is a *third* approach to life, to discovering meaning in life. The witness of Ezekiel to his people in exile and of Paul to the Christians of Rome, is that — despite all appearances to the contrary — God's desire for the people is not that death overcome life as may appear to be the case, but that life overcome death.

Ezekiel must have seen it in a vision from God. No one who had been part of a culture that had been utterly annihilated, who had seen the entire people carried off from their land, their crops burned, their children murdered, their king blinded before the people's eyes, then sent to live among the slums of Babylon, no one, having seen all that, could say a word like:

I will put my Spirit within you, and you shall live,
And I will place you in your own land; then you shall
know that I, the Lord, have spoken ...

... not unless he had been party to a vision from God. It was a vision that convinced him that the God of Israel, despite utterly hopeless circumstances — unlike anything you or I could ever have seen — this God will give to the people a life that only God can give. Ezekiel, amid circumstances of almost unimaginable hopelessness, was moved to utter a word of hope. And hope in the strongest terms. A valley of dead skeletons returned to life through the agency of the prophet and by the power of God. God wills life for God's people, and as Ezekiel gave us a view of what that means for the People of Israel, for Christians Paul said:

If the Spirit of him who raised Jesus from the dead
dwells in you,
He who raised Jesus Christ from the dead will give life
to your
mortal bodies also through his Spirit which dwells in
you.

"He will give life to you in your mortal bodies also." Not just "pie in the sky by and by," not just a spirit time some time after death; but God will give life, the empowering spirit of life, not just in a future time, but now. Isn't it ironic? To set our minds on the flesh, living for this life, leads to death. But somehow, to live in Christ promises not only life in the hereafter, but the first experience of truly living in the present that we can have.

Once a major magazine interviewed people over 100 with the question, "When did you cease being young?" The average answer given was eighty, and the youngest answer given was sixty! The fact of the matter is that every day is a gift of God, whether it comes after 100 or after twenty. It is whether that gift of life is lived in the presence of Christ that determines whether we are truly alive, or just biding our time until our time ends.

Slaving After Freedom

Preachers often wonder what to do with Palm Sunday. Frequently the day is given to a celebration of Jesus' triumphal procession into Jerusalem.

Sometimes, though, worship provides a different offering, given the alternate title of Passion Sunday, leaving behind the pomp and celebration of Palm Sunday for a hard look at the events of the coming week, the last supper, the betrayal, the crucifixion, the burial in the tomb. It is because we know about the passion that is coming that preachers always wonder what to do with the happy celebration of Palm Sunday.

A friend in Pennsylvania,[1] responding to the question, "What are you doing for your Palm Sunday sermon?" wrote:

> *I'm thinking of beginning the sermon this way:*
> *It looked like a parade. There was a center stretch for somebody important to walk. The enthusiastic crowds gathered on both sides, craning their necks to see ... Abuzz with excitement, people thronged to see someone who could redeem them from [their] ordinary humdrum lives. The air was charged with politics, as some wondered, "Is this the moment when our hero will speak out on some important issue?" Suddenly, an anxious voice rang out — "Look! Somebody's coming!" Every single head in that crowd turned with anticipation ... and a limousine pulled up, and actress Sharon Stone got out.*

43

She was the Hero(-ine) everybody wanted, six days
before Palm Sunday, a vision in blond, a glamorous
star ... her torso adorned the cover of People *maga-*
zine ... She was interviewed by Barbara Walters. And
with one billion people watching one Monday night,
with adoring fans waving microphones like palm
branches, Sharon Stone made her grand entrance into
the Academy Awards.

In some ways, that parade was the embodiment of
the American dream. And she did it the old fashioned
way, leaving the small city of Meadville, Pennsylva-
nia, and going to someplace better. "I couldn't wait to
get out of that dreary little town," she told Barbara
Walters. And now, she has made it ...

... [Once there was] another scene that looked like
a parade. The crowd was smaller, say the scholars, but
every bit as enthusiastic. Instead of a limousine, Jesus
arrived on a flea-bitten donkey. Instead of going to
receive an award, Jesus rode on "in lowly pomp ... to
die." Instead of leaving his small town roots, an early
hymn of the church (Philippians 2) tells us that he spent
his time in small, lowly places ... He set his face like
flint ... to give his life away.

Palm Sunday and Easter are so very different, separated by a
wide week of suffering and death. The difference between Palm
Sunday and Easter is something like the little boy who had a ticket
to the circus, who went into town and saw the great parade of
wagons, clowns, and exotic animals, and then went home because
he thought that having seen the parade, he had seen the circus. We
know this isn't so. And if we think about it at all, we know Palm
Sunday is not a little Easter. In churches where children receive
palms to wave, they soon weave them into crosses. This is where
Palm Sunday is headed, toward the cross.

Why is this so? Paul had an answer to that question. He said
that though Jesus was in the form of God, he set that aside in order
to empty himself, take the form of a slave, and be born as a human
person. He said Jesus became the sort of servant for whom a call

44

to face death was not regarded as too great a task for one seeking to be faithful.

What does it mean to be a slave or a servant — it's the same word in the original language — who is willing to be obedient even to death? Few of us would have any idea. The "Suffering Servant"[2] of Isaiah is the prime Old Testament witness to the calling to pursue freedom through servanthood.

Hearing The Word Of God

Isaiah said, "Morning by morning he wakens — wakens my ear to listen as those who are taught. The Lord God has opened my ear, and I was not rebellious ..." Have you ever thought about the need for our ears to be "wakened"? Some married folks often wonder how their spouses can sleep through their own snoring. It's easy, their ears are asleep along with the rest of them! What an image for preparing to hear the Word God has to say to us: that God wakens our ears to hear. Before telling, God makes us ready to hear. We may think our ears work fine already, but think how often our preset opinions block out a new thing God would have us hear. We are so accustomed to listening for what we already think that a new word might well pass us by, it's just not familiar enough.

Fred Craddock, professor of preaching, once wrote about one of his students who entered seminary after working with people who were hearing impaired. The student described an incident from his work that took place on the Monday after Thanksgiving. Seven-year-old Heather had ears that worked just fine, but for some reason the words she heard never made it to her brain. He took her by the shoulders and asked, "Heather ... what did you eat for Thanksgiving? What did you have for Thanksgiving dinner, Heather?" Heather broke into a beautiful smile and said, "My shoes are red." She simply could not hear. Dr. Craddock went on:

> *Heather's problem was pathological, but what often happens in church is just as tragic. I was in Dallas, Texas, on a Sunday morning and worshiped at the church nearest my hotel. It turned out to be one of those*

rare, glorious experiences when the hymns, the anthem,
the scripture readings, the sermon, the prayers, and
the fellowship combined to bless me richly. The chem-
istry was right, or perhaps I was just right in my need.
After the benediction I stood where I was, almost im-
mobilized. A man in the pew in front of me turned
around and said, "Do you think Tom Landry is going
to coach any more?" In other words, this man was
saying to me, "My shoes are red."[3]

Remember the old story about the man with beans in his ears? His friend tells him, "You've got beans in your ears," but he responds, "What?" So his friend repeats his words a little more loudly, "I said, you've got beans in your ears." But the man responds again, "What?" So the friend shouts now, *"You've got beans in your ears!"* and the man responds, "Sorry, I can't hear you, I've got beans in my ears." It's a silly story that points out two things: our need to hear, but also that often the very thing we need to hear is something we already know. Like the commercial for corn flakes that urges us to taste them again for the first time, many times the words of our faith are something we need to hear again for the first time.

I have a friend who once received a letter from another friend who is a pastor. He was preaching his way through the three-year cycle of scripture that many of us use to organize our preaching. By the time he reached his seventh year of ministry, he had been through the readings twice before. He wrote to ask what my friend thought he should do. This was going to be his third time through the same readings. His question makes us think, "How many times have I heard the parable of the prodigal son? How often have I been instructed by the incomparable words of the Sermon on the Mount? How important is it to remind ourselves of the truth of John 3:16, that God loved the world enough to send a savior to us?" My friend remembered writing to him something like, "The difference between hearing and hearing again is not as great as we might think. Those very same worshipers have heard many of those Bible passages long before you began reading them with them." When God opens our ears, as Isaiah said, it may not be something entirely new that we are to hear, but something familiar that strikes us in a new way this time around.

One of the significant aspects of discipleship involves hearing the Word of God, even if, as in the traumatic events of Holy Week, that Word seems destined to shake us up.

Doing The Word Of God

The letter of James is the one that declares that faith without works is just about as good as no faith at all. One of the jokes making the rounds of churches these days has a person dying and finding himself in hell. He looks around and sees Martin Luther and John Calvin standing nearby. He is deeply troubled. His own life was not that exemplary, but how can these two great figures of the Reformation have found themselves on the wrong side of the Pearly Gates? So he asks them. Calvin responds, "I'm afraid it's some bad news, really. Apparently works *do* matter."

Coming to church, hearing about the content of our faith, is part of the disciple's task. It is good to know the content of the truth about salvation. But opening our minds to that truth is only half the disciple's task. Knowing the work of salvation rightly leads to doing the work of salvation. Isaiah wrote words concerning the work of discipleship which line up so readily with our anticipation of the events of Holy Week: "I have set my face like flint, and I know that I shall not be put to shame." "Jesus set his face like flint — to give his life away." Jesus has been described in many ways, but one appealing way is as "a man for others." How does that square up with a descriptive phrase like, "I have set my face like flint"? It means that his course to the cross, though made in humility, was undeterred. A self-emptying servant who taught and lived the truth that greatness comes only in service, true greatness resides in those who give of themselves without thought of return.

In his excellent recent biography of Harry Truman, David McCullough tells the story of the President from Missouri. After being elected to the office of Vice President, which he did not seek, and two months later being thrust into the office of the Presidency where he was faced with some of the most gripping decisions to face any leader in our century — the atomic bomb, the post-war

Potsdam Conference, the war in Korea, the surprise reelection to office against all odds — even after all the trappings of office which had held him bound like a prisoner in a gilded cage, when he handed over the keys to Eisenhower, he wanted nothing much more than to return to Independence, Missouri, and take up the life of a private citizen again. Of course, it wasn't so simple to do that. Things never are that simple. But he did return to the home in which he and his wife had lived before he was anybody. Even his detractors would say that Truman was a man who gave of himself selflessly.

One illustration of that stands out. Alden Whitman of *The New York Times* had been assigned the task of writing Truman's obituary when the time came. Anyone with such an assignment for such a publication makes sure to have most of what he wants to say prepared long before it is needed. When Whitman went to Independence to interview Truman, "feeling extremely uneasy about the whole assignment, Truman greeted him with a smile, saying, 'I know why you're here and I want to help you all I can.'"[4] Doing the Word of God involves an attitude of self-giving service which itself is an unequaled gift of God to those who would follow Christ.

This coming week represents the church's annual celebration of the greatness of the gift of Christ to the world. The tragedy of it is that many will not hear. On Good Friday, when Christians worship together and recall the cost of the servanthood of Jesus, in many churches there will be but a handful present compared to those on the bandwagon on Easter morning. It is so often this way. Yet it is so hard to live the life of resurrection unless we have first heard the truth about the cost of salvation.

Anyone planning to go to only one service during Holy Week should give serious thought to attending a service on Good Friday. It can be a time that leads us through death into a fuller appreciation of the resurrected life in Christ on Easter morning.

---

1. Bill Carter, pastor of the First Presbyterian Church, Clarks Summit, Pennsylvania.

2. The four "Suffering Servant Songs" in Isaiah are 1) 42:1-9; 2) 49:1-6; 3) 50:4-9a; 4) 52:13—53:12.

3. "The Preacher And The Preaching," *Reformed Review*, Autumn, 1990.

4. David McCullough, *Truman* (Simon & Schuster, 1992), p. 990.

Maundy Thursday
Exodus 12:1-4 (5-10) 11-14

For And Against

Reading over the Exodus account of the institution of the Passover, we discover important resources for preparing our hearts and minds for the holy meal we are about to celebrate. In the old days, some denominations required the use of little wooden or metal buttons called "communion tokens" which were handed out the week before the Lord's Supper was to be celebrated. These were supposed to serve as certification for admission to the Lord's table on the following week. The leaders of some churches made it their business to keep very close track of those who failed to participate, and also to see to it that "unfit" people were not permitted to commune.

The majority of churches have discontinued this practice, for the most part. One of the reasons is that we are aware of different needs in modern circumstances. Members of congregations are on the move continually, and so we couldn't count on the fact that a token handed out one week would be used in the same sanctuary the next. But there is a more important reason. Just as we can't count on the presence of the same folks from week to week, we wouldn't want to limit access to the table only to those who are active members of our own congregation. In the Invitation at the table we hear words such as: "Our Savior invites those who trust in him to come and share in the feast which he has prepared." Now, Jesus does not invite just this church or that denomination, but all those who trust in him. That means that the table is pretty open to anyone and everyone whose life is in the process of responding to the call of Christ.

What does the Passover have to do with all this? A good deal. Frequently, the temptation in the church has been to overly spiritualize the sacrament. The insistence of 1,000,000 sermons since New Testament times — that the deliverance of God is a spiritual matter — must run up against the Old Testament feast of the Passover, which serves as the foundation for our celebration of the Lord's Supper. Our insistence that God's liberation is spiritual does not cancel the Old Testament witness that the physical freedom of people is involved as well. This does not narrow the importance of the realm of the spirit, but rather enhances it. Perhaps it enhances our understanding of the "spirit" in unexpected ways.

Dr. Roy Fairchild of San Francisco Theological Seminary once asked a large convocation audience to call out words that came to their minds when they heard the word "spiritual." "Piety," "meditation," "holy" were the sort of words that came in response. Then he said, "What words come to mind when you hear the word "spirited"? Now folks thought of words such as "lively," "animated," "energetic."

What was the difference? In actual fact, the word *spirited* is a more faithful biblical concept than our current understanding of *spiritual*. Our faith must not be conceived as a spiritual matter, so much as it is a spirited one. That throws the entire idea of such things as the Lord's Supper into a whole new light. When we forget our Passover roots in the Lord's Supper, we can become excessively spiritual about it, forget that God really intends to free real people. We can sit as isolated, even mournful-looking individuals in our pews, partaking of a sacrament that seems almost ludicrous when we think of the actual meaning of a word like *communion*: that it is *community* with God and each other which we celebrate at the table.

I hope we can begin to think of the celebration of the Lord's Supper as a spirited experience, enlivened by the spirit of God. Now, don't fret, there will be no introduction of parlor games into worship in order to make the sacrament more lively. Still, I would like for each worshiper to consider not only his or her relationship to God which we declare in taking the sacrament, but the new relationship with each other which Jesus' sacred meal makes possible. The Passover, as we will remember, was a distinctly social occasion, even though fraught with anxiety the first night it was celebrated. The Passover was not a time for each child of Israel to retire to his or her room and contemplate spiritual matters. Rather, it was a spirited occasion celebrated in households while people ate and drank together — as it is to this day in Jewish homes — in anticipation of God's saving act of liberation.

When Jesus established the sacrament of the Lord's Supper, it was not alone in his room, but at this very Passover meal, with his family of disciples. Ever since it has been a means whereby the people of the church have declared the continuing presence of Christ in our midst. The Passover serves as a warning against overlooking the community in which we are gathered when we call ourselves a church. Both the Passover and the Lord's Supper look to the past to find hope for the future.

Having recognized all this, like the people of Israel who first heard Moses' instructions concerning the Passover, we may wonder at its power. Can we really believe that God has the power to overcome the evils that seem so much more present to us than the promise of our deliverance? We hear the words of the prophet Moses, but we see the power of Pharaoh and all his army standing between us and our freedom. Even if God in Christ is a powerful ally to us, is Christ strong enough to fortify us when the evils of the world seem so much more apparent? Paul asked the same questions when he wrote to the Christians in Rome.

"Who shall separate us from the love of Christ?" Paul came up with a convincing list (Romans 8:31-39). Still, no matter the obstacles the world might raise, regardless of tribulation, persecution, powers, even our own self-destructive behavior, Paul declared that God is still for us more than anything else can possibly be against us.

That is what blood on the doorposts comes down to. That is what crucifixion comes down to. That is what symbolic meals shared around tables such as this one and real meals shared around other tables of love in our homes and gatherings come down to. That is what helpless armies of Pharaoh and other superpowers come down to. That is what the smallest act of kindness and the largest sacrifice we can make for others come down to. They all lead to the self same conclusion as the one reached with such dynamic intensity by Paul: the One who is for us is so very much more the wave of the future than all the evils that may line up against us that we may rejoice even if we must rejoice in adversity.

Friends, believe the Good News of the gospel: nothing in the whole wide world can separate us from the love of God in Christ Jesus our Lord. Thanks be to God, who gives us the victory!

Atonement: At-One-Ment

See, my servant shall prosper;
he shall be exalted and lifted up.

Not long ago, I read about a pastor who was visiting a neighboring church as the guest speaker for their women's group. As he
sat through the preliminaries of the meeting, he discovered that
the group had an odd little ritual, something they called the "Bible
verse roll call." They had all promised each other that they would
memorize a verse of scripture each month. As they went through
the names in alphabetical order, the respondents would answer by
saying aloud the Bible verse that they had memorized. There was
no particular rhyme or reason to the verses chosen, so there were
bits from both testaments, from the Gospels, from the letters, from
the Psalms. At the end of the roll was a woman whose last name
began with a Y. She was the only person there who had forgotten
to memorize a scripture verse, "So, with a red face and a shaky
voice, she stood up and recited that great scriptural ace in the hole:
'Jesus wept.'[1] There was good-natured laughter. We often laugh
about that verse."[2]

But the verse isn't funny, is it? Weeping. Nothing very funny
about that. No kind of weeping is very funny, unless you just happen to be laughing until you cry. And perhaps not even then. But
it's not just the weeping, it's the one who is doing the weeping.
Jesus wept. Jesus. Son of God. Chosen one. The beloved in whom
God was well-pleased. And in the story where "Jesus wept," he
was weeping because someone had died. Where before there had

55

been life and vitality and good company and all the things that friendship provides, now there remained only the ravages left behind after a death.

The opening verse of our passage for today is stunningly out of place alongside the remainder of the poem, almost as out of place as laughter alongside a verse that says, "Jesus wept."

"See, my servant shall prosper; he shall be exalted and lifted up" is set right alongside these words: "so marred was his appearance ... he had no form or majesty that we should look at him." It is rather like our Palm Sunday parades of joy in the face of that which awaits Jesus here at the end of the week. It is jarring, hard to reconcile the two. Dissonance seems an apt musical sort of description.

I can almost hear the tuneful and hopeful "Hosanna, Loud Hosanna" being sung or played alongside a dirge, or a minor-mode cacophony of train whistles and jackhammers. Or a medleying of that most somber Lenten hymn, "Go To Dark Gethsemane" right alongside our bright and happy "All Glory Laud and Honor" (which one of my friends insists on calling "All Glory, *Loud* and Honor"). The one tune, rather smug and self-satisfied, ebullient, being knocked off its pins by the insistence of the other's unyielding horror.

Every year at this time, I notice a phenomenon characteristic of the churches in which I have worshiped and served. You could phrase it this way: While everybody wants to come for the pot roast, very few want to be there when they butcher the cow. We live most of our lives very far removed from hosts of sacrifices that take place on a daily basis in order to provide us with what we need to eat and to wear. In order for us to eat the hamburger or wear the leather coat, some creature must lose its life. In order for us to have roads and highways and houses, some creatures must lose their habitat. In order for us to be safe on our streets and in our homes, some police officers and fire fighters must stay up all night. If the power goes out in the middle of the night during a storm, we wouldn't think it was just fine if all the power company people finished their night's sleep before going out to see about fixing the problem. If we think about it, we could make a long list of sacrifices made on our behalf every day. These are all meant to bring us closer to the kind of life we want to have, to some sort of ideal. The fact that such sacrifices escape our awareness most of the time doesn't make it any less true that they are sacrifices made for our sakes.

The suffering which the Servant of God experienced in the passage from Isaiah was clearly such a sacrifice for others. The others say as much, when they declare, "Surely he has borne *our* infirmities and carried *our* diseases ... he was wounded for *our* transgressions, crushed for *our* iniquities" (italics added).

So, we arrive at one of the deepest of questions that our faith sets before us. It is difficult to understand, that suffering and death of one person somehow makes clear the path for another. How can the suffering of one alleviate the need for suffering by another? The very fact that the topic touches on suffering, that alone is enough to keep people out of the church in droves on a day like Good Friday. Who wants to dwell on such things? Yet, while we may wonder at this idea, may even choose to avoid it, we do discover that there is something to it, even in the plainest human experiences. The parent who sacrifices for years so that a child may be the first in their family to graduate from college — this is an experience of the transforming power of one person's actions in the life of another. In the poem in Isaiah, the same sort of human capacity to recognize a selfless gift of one for another is recognized.

The word for the sort of suffering about which we read in Isaiah is *atonement*. Atonement is one of those theological words that gets a workout on seminary campuses and in religion classes in colleges, but it doesn't often work its way into everyday conversation, does it? We might think our boss or our neighbor or our spouse has a lot to atone for, but we don't often phrase it just that way. Lots of times, in those academic-sounding conversations, it comes with a special modifier: *substitutionary* atonement.

Atonement is simply a fancy pronunciation for two words and a suffix: "at-one-ment." Atonement is any action by which things or people that were separated become reconciled. One person, having offended his friend by some unfortunate word, finds they are no longer at one, no longer enjoying the benefits of common minds and hearts. Atonement is necessary and may come in the form of an apology, a gift, some gesture that reaches toward the other. And, if it works out right; the two may be friends again; atonement may be accomplished.

Substitutionary atonement simply means that if we find ourselves beyond hope of reconciliation with the one from whom we are estranged, there may be a way that a third party can stand in the breach and help us toward atonement. The substitute may be like a chemical catalyst, so that the two materials which have separated and cannot join under their own power, may, by office of the catalyst, be made one again.

Christian preachers have, for centuries, seen in the suffering servant of Isaiah, a prefiguring of the suffering which Jesus undertook for our sakes. He stood in our place; as Isaiah says, "He was wounded for our transgressions." Jesus placed his very life in the vice grip of death so that we might be made pure enough to approach the throne of God.

As Jesus rode into Jerusalem on Palm Sunday, he was riding toward his appointment as a substitutionary atonement for the sins of the world. He was on his way to being bruised for our sakes, for being despised and rejected, for undertaking the punishment that rightfully belonged to those who accused him, both then and in all the generations that have lived before or since. That is what he was on his way to become, a substitutionary atonement, standing in as a substitute for us, that we might be "at one" with God again.

I recently read about a farmer who was asked what it was like to grow up on the farm and provide their own food.[3] She reported that raising and eating their own vegetables was no problem. But she said providing meat was difficult. She told the story of taking a young calf to the slaughterhouse. The calf became frightened, so her father rode in the back of the trailer with the calf to keep it calm. By the time they arrived, her father was in tears, because the trusting and innocent calf had been licking his arm the whole way.

One dies that others may live. It is a hard thing for us to consider, but no less true because it is hard. We would rather look the other way, think on more pleasant things. But this is the day that

58

comes around to remind us just how costly the atonement for our sins was and is.

After this day, we will remember that these two things go together: "Surely ... he was wounded for *our* transgressions, crushed for *our* iniquities." and "See, my servant shall prosper; he shall be exalted and lifted up."

In the end, he is at one with with God. And because of him, in the end, we are too.

---

1. John 11:35, though the NRSV spoils all the fun, rendering it, "Jesus began to weep."

2. Theodore Wardlaw, "When Jesus Wept," *Journal For Preachers*, Lent 2000, p. 36.

3. Barbara Brown Taylor, "In The Name Of Law And Order," *Home By Another Way* (Cowley Publications, 1999), p. 86.

Pastor, It's Cornelius On The Line ...

There stood Peter, in the very position in which lots of believers have found themselves. It could happen on an airplane, across the desk at work, over the backyard fence, at the laundry with a neighbor from the apartment next door, even with a member of our own family. Someone says, "What do you think the deal is about Jesus, anyway?" or "What goes on at your church for people like me?" or even, "Sometimes I wonder if there even is a God, don't you?"

Some call this Peter's "sermon" in Cornelius' house. I've read it over many times, and it doesn't look like much of a sermon to me. Where is the funny story that is supposed to start things off? Where is the poem by Longfellow at the end? And, of course, it's way too short. No, this is more like a response to a question from a friend. It's as if Cornelius called Peter one day to ask to borrow his lawn mower, and their conversation drifted off into more serious matters, until Cornelius finally said, "Say, Peter, you knew that guy Jesus. What was the deal with him, anyway?" What Peter said is really a story, more than a sermon.

The story comes with three parts:

Part One was the part before Peter had anything to do with the story. Family histories are like that: The days when Great-Grandad came from Sweden on the boat with just the clothes he was wearing, or when Great-Aunt Maggie came west across the prairie with the wagons, or when Grandad dodged bullets as he led his fleeing family across the river into Thailand. Family history is like that; though we may not have been present for all the events, we feel a part of them somehow. The grandparents of a friends of mine came to this country from Scotland, another set was already here, and one thing led to another, all happening before my friend was around to affect the course of events, 'til one day he was born. But our family histories are no less a part of us or less determinative of who we are for our not having been present for part of the story. They are like rivers, running before we encountered them, continuing after we are no longer in them.

That is what the first part of Peter's story was like. He spoke first of the people of Israel. Peter was a Jew, the people of Israel were his people, but they had a long history dating back to the patriarchs, back to the Exodus, back to King David and King Solomon and Noah and Jonah and Job and Ruth and Naomi and Abraham and Sarah, and an additional cast of thousands, all of whom had an impact on the story long before Peter, the fisherman from Galilee, came on the scene. Nevertheless, he knew that that story was his story, it was about his people, it was a story of the many ways in which God had worked in the past to save them and make them a people who would be a blessing for the whole world.

Part Two of Peter's story is the main part. It could have begun with Peter saying, "And by the time I met Jesus, here is what was happening ..." He just tells in very brief fashion his own experiences of the way he came to know who Jesus was and what Jesus did that made him so special. They came across sick people and, just when you'd least expect it, "poof" they were healed, because Jesus was so filled with the power and presence of God. Peter's story also tells the hard part, the part the church has rehearsed again through the week just past, the part where Jesus was arrested and put to death on a cross. But then — who could have guessed it, though considering all they had seen with him, they had to wonder why they were surprised — God raised Jesus from death! And those who followed knew beyond a doubt that he was alive and with them, and every time they sat down together to break bread, doggone if they couldn't just feel him there as they used to before he was crucified!

And so, something had to be done, they couldn't just keep news like this to themselves. So they began telling others what had happened. And they began opening their Bibles and suddenly — why hadn't they seen it before? — it looked as though words about who Jesus was and is were spread all over every page. Everywhere they looked they saw something that made them think of him and what he had done and what he was still doing among them.

So they began telling the story to others. They even began telling it to people like Cornelius, who hadn't been part of the family, but it seemed like the right thing to do.

(3) *Part Three* of Peter's story is the part that really changes things. It is the future part of the story, the part that in the fairy tales would simply say, "And they lived happily ever after." But the future of this story, "The Story of Jesus and How He Changed My Life," was more inviting than that. Peter began invitationally saying, "I truly understand that God shows no partiality," and ended the same way with, "everyone who believes in him receives forgiveness in his name ..." Paul wrote much the same thing in fancier words in Romans 8: "If we know the love of Jesus, we have come to realize that nothing can separate us from the love of God." In other words, Peter tells Cornelius and all the folks in his house who are gathered there that his story can become their story too. That's how it is with the best stories anyway, isn't it? We finish by feeling as though the author had said something true about us as well as the folks in his story. That's the way Peter ends. This story is for us.

Easter is that strange season for the church when those of us who have been hanging around these doors for the past twelve months are called to remember that the story is not just for us, at least not for us alone. The story of Jesus Christ is only a living story inasmuch as we tell it as Peter did, as we finish by inviting Cornelius into the flow of the action so the story can go on. When the phone rings the week before Easter and some stranger on the other end asks, "What time does mass begin at your church, father?" I have to remember it is Cornelius on the line. This is especially important if the person is speaking to one of the women who has served on our pastoral staff, whom no one would mistake for anybody's father! This is someone who perhaps doesn't know all the customs of our church but who is ready to hear the story.

More than that, it is often someone hoping to find where he or she might have a part to play in that story. Every one of us has at one time been in Cornelius' shoes. Perhaps some of us here today are in his shoes right now, on the outside of the story, looking for a part to play.

A few years ago, when Billy Graham came to hold a crusade in Portland, Oregon, a friend of mine happened to sit next to someone who had been in the audience the last time Dr. Graham had been in Portland, forty years before. After the sermon, my friend turned to this person and asked what he thought. His response was surprising. First, he said, it was virtually the same sermon he had heard forty years before. Then he said, here is the part that was so surprising, "Isn't that great?"

Great? Great that he hasn't thought of a new thing to say in forty years? No, great that he is still telling the story, the same story, as a way of inviting people to become part of it, carrying on the story-telling with all those Corneliuses outside the church family which Peter began doing so long ago, inviting people in, telling us we can become part of it.

To all of us, Peter's words are still true: "God shows no partiality ... everyone who believes in him receives forgiveness through his name." The church is not a place where we earn our stripes and strive to earn God's love. The only reason we are together at Easter is because Jesus has made us into a fellowship of the forgiven and newly acceptable. That makes us ready and able to play the part in the story God that has in mind for us.

Surely there is someone here today who has come hoping for a word that lets you know that you belong, that the story we rehearse here week after week is also your story. Well, here is that word. Believe in Jesus and accept salvation in his name. Do that with me as we pray, and you will find it is just the beginning of a whole new chapter in the amazing story of faith.

Peter's Story: Our Story

Frederick Buechner described Peter's vigil outside the high priest's place on the night of Jesus' arrest this way:

> *"Listen," [Jesus] said, "the cock won't crow till you've betrayed me three times," and that's the way it was, of course — Peter sitting out there in the high priest's courtyard keeping warm by the fire while, inside, the ghastly interrogation was in process, and then the girl coming up to ask him three times if he wasn't one of them and his replying each time that he didn't know what in God's name she was talking about. And then the old cock's wattles trembling scarlet as up over the horizon it squawked the rising sun, and the tears running down Peter's face like rain down a rock.* [1]

By any reckoning, it's a long journey from that sorry courtyard denial to the day in Jerusalem when Peter stood up before God and everybody to declare himself for this man Jesus. How did he get from here to there? How could we get there too? Would we want to? These questions pestered the people milling about Jerusalem that day. They ought to pester us as well.

In the Sundays of Easter this year there are seven selections from the books of Acts. That may sound like a lot, but consider this — Luke reports 28 speeches in Acts all together — that's four times the number we have in our lectionary! Lloyd Ogilvie wrote a well-known and — if many libraries' well-thumbed copies are any indication — well-loved volume[2] that has 26 chapters on this single New Testament book. On a bookshelf in his study, a pastor friend of mine has five commentaries on Acts. Obviously, it is a New Testament book with much to say to us, for so many are listening to its words and writing about them for others. And, like so many of the Gospel stories, it is Peter who, speaking for all the disciples, said what needed to be said, or asked what needed to be asked.

Acts picks up where the Gospel of Luke leaves off, and was written by the same person. But what a change takes place from one volume to the next! At the close of the Gospel of Luke, some of the disciples have seen the resurrected Jesus, and they have busily shared the news with others. Then Jesus appeared to them and spoke to them of things in scripture, reminding them that they were witnesses to the momentous events of Holy Week in Jerusalem. The final verse of Luke's Gospel has the disciples in Jerusalem continually in the temple blessing God, but apparently keeping most of the news about Jesus to themselves.

At the beginning of Acts, we see Jesus with the disciples again, physically present for the last time, telling them, "You shall be my witnesses in Jerusalem and in all Judea and Samaria and to the end of the earth." As it turns out, this was not so much a command to be obeyed, but a trustworthy promise. At the very moment in which he said it, even given the excitement of the resurrection, we can just imagine disciples like Peter wondering to themselves, "Wherever will I find the inner courage to be such a witness?" — especially one who could not make himself constant for even the one night of the cross. How was he then to become a faithful witness to his fellow Jews, to foreigners like Samaritans, and even to Gentiles whose language and culture he neither knew nor particularly appreciated?

All those questions were set aside by the empowering Holy Spirit that came upon them. No one knows for sure how many days passed between one of these events and the other. It doesn't matter. What matters is that the disciples were given a gospel to which they were to be witnesses, and they were given a power quite outside themselves by which to become witnesses to that gospel. How do the weak become strong? How did the mute ones of Good Friday become the public proclaimers of Pentecost Day? In particular, how did Peter cease to feel like a betrayer and begin to feel like an apostle?

It is really through Peter's sermon that all this becomes clear. While it wasn't a sermon as we may be accustomed to sermons — three main points, poem, humorous story at the beginning — it was still every bit a sermon, a proclamation of the Good News. He chose for his text Psalm 16. It was a perfect choice, really. As you may or may not know, there is little hope about a life after death expressed in the Old Testament. The standard belief was in a shadowy sort of post-death existence called Sheol. But Psalm 16 represents an Old Testament breakthrough. And it achieves its new point of view because of the poet's sense of intimacy with God.

The Psalm describes the faith of one who has, through his life, come to feel so intimately connected with God, so accompanied by God on his every step in life, that he cannot imagine a God so concerned about him and so faithful to him to be a God who would ultimately abandon him to death. Peter hastened to point out that David — whom tradition held to be the author of all the Psalms — did not fully inherit the promise of this Psalm, since his tomb was present even in their day, and anyone who wanted to could take a short walk through Jerusalem and go see it. The poet must have been writing of someone else. And Jesus, descended through the line of David, was the one. His tomb could not be found. Or rather, his body was gone and no one could produce it. The tomb of a dead King David, and the empty tomb of the Messiah Jesus were set alongside one another in Peter's sermon. But that's not all.

Having made this declaration that Jesus — the wonder worker they had all seen in Jerusalem — was claimed by scripture itself as the Messiah of God, it became shatteringly evident to the gathered crowd that when they had shouted for the death of Jesus, they had called for the death of God's chosen one, they had received God's messenger and had murdered him. Luke reported that at the end of Peter's sermon, they were cut to the heart. That's a vivid way of describing a heartbreak.

Their hearts were cut, they were bleeding spiritually. The One God had sent to heal them they had murdered; the One in whom the hope of the world was present had now been sent packing from the world. Once we have killed the very hope that lives among or within us, where will hope then be found? Isn't that the mark of a dead end, a life at the point of last resort, a people finally cut off from their own souls? What was there for them to do? All seemed hopeless, for even hope seemed to be lost.

You have known people who have done this. You hear them speaking all the time. "I know I really should do such and such, but I just never do." "I really should eat better and get exercise, but I never get to it," they say as their health deteriorates before our very eyes. "I really should take more time for my family, but right now I'm up to here at work," they say as precious moments slip away forever. "Perhaps I'll get to the things I really love doing once I retire," they say as the activities for which they are fit today slip silently away. In a thousand ways, we may not exactly be killing the Messiah, but we throw away the extravagant gifts of God to us as though we had all the time in the world, all the health to squander, all the resources to set aside for a time that never comes. Till one day we wake up and wonder why the remainder of our lives seems so crowded into a corner, why the openness and happiness and joy of our lives seems to have left us, and all we have is a sense of a remaining time that desperately needs hoarding.

Having killed the savior, we are powerless to save ourselves. No wonder the crowd cried out to Peter in despair, "What shall we do?" They truly didn't know. And when we get right down to it, there are so many times in our lives when we don't know either.

Now Peter answered, "Repent and be baptized in the name of Jesus Christ for the forgiveness of sins." That can sound to modern ears like a line from a tent revival meeting, but it is as desperately needed today as in any day. It is just that the familiarity of the language has caused us to think of it as quaint and old fashioned. But what is repentance? It isn't a command to say we are sorry. It isn't a demand for an apology, as though some groveling regret could ever bring back the savior they had thrown away.

Repentance literally means to turn around. Charging toward hell at seventy miles per hour, the evangelist Peter urges his listeners to make a 180-degree turn. This isn't just a change of mind, or a softening of the heart, but a turning around of life. Where before it had been work, goods, social relationships, sports, music, or whatever that had claimed top priority in life, Peter says it is time to be claimed by another priority, and be baptized in his name. While modern life often makes it seem as though the choice to follow Jesus is one of many great choices we are called upon to make in life, the sermon Peter preached makes it evident that without the choice for Jesus, all other choices are ultimately scarred and misshapen, no matter what our good intentions may be. With repentance and a turn toward Christ, is life. Without it is death. It is not a choice among equally valid choices; it is a choice without which there will cease to be other choices.

As Albert Winn, fine Southern Presbyterian preacher, once said, the news Peter delivers is not for sentiment or entertainment or curiosity, but to drive people into a corner where they must either believe and obey this Lord or reject him.[3] Life cannot go on as it was. That urgency has not changed today. Christ has done something unique in the world, quite apart from our own striving, and our all-too-often striving against him. We cannot ignore it. We must take sides. Peter calls on his listeners to side with Jesus. Three thousand chose to do so that very day. And that was only the beginning. As far as he knew right then, the gospel was only going to help renew Israel. Peter had no idea yet that Gentiles would one day be welcomed into the fellowship of Jesus the Messiah. The Spirit had only begun with the church. New things were to come cascading down in great heaping splashes. In coming chapters there would be Gentiles baptized, the greatest persecutor of the church would turn his life around and become the world's greatest evangelist, kings would find their way to the throne of grace, even Gentiles would become preachers and evangelists themselves.

The Spirit was hardly finished with surprises on that first day, and it is hardly finished with us today. So if you find in your heart that the Spirit is calling you in a special way, won't you take the time to listen? Our Bible says Peter told them, "Save yourselves," but it would be better translated, "Let yourselves be saved!" That is what the Spirit has in mind for you if you are feeling that nudge today. Jesus has you in mind — always has. The sermon title is an encouragement to see it that way: "Peter's Story: Our Story." They are very much alike, really. We — like Peter — have things about which to repent — but even so, we can be witnesses. From traitor to witness in one day is a long leap, but Christ has that in mind. Christ has us in mind for his kingdom every bit as much as he had in mind Peter and the throngs in Jerusalem that day. All he really needs is our go-ahead to make all the difference in the meaning behind the lives we are living. Let's give him that today. Our fellowship will be all the richer for it, and our witness in our community will come to life in a whole new way.

The Acts of the Apostles might better be called the Acts of the Holy Spirit, since it is the Spirit that really empowers everything that takes place in this wonderful book. And that is just what the Holy Spirit can do among us: bring life such as few of us may have dreamed possible.

1. Frederick Buechner, *Peculiar Treasures: A Biblical Who's Who* (Harper & Row, 1979), p. 136.

2. Lloyd Ogilvie, *Drumbeat Of Love* (Word Books, 1976).

3. Albert C. Winn, *The Layman's Bible Commentary: Acts Of The Apostles,* Vol. 20 (Louisville: John Knox Press, 1961), p. 39.

To Be Lord, To Be Messiah,
To Be Crucified

Think of all the ways in which we hold ourselves at a distance from people and things that come near to us. We may not think about it very often, but we do it all the time. As a friend of mine was walking into town the other day, he passed by a woman who was plopped down in the sunshine on the sidewalk, wearing disheveled clothing, smoking a cigarette. She eyed him evaluatively. He looked straight ahead, not really wanting to make eye contact, glad he had on his sunglasses, not wanting to have to respond to a request for spare change. She didn't speak and neither did he. Though he claims to value relationships more highly than just about anything, he does not always seek them, not in every circumstance. He passed by. At a distance.

Not long ago that same friend was speaking with a parent who was wondering how it was that she ever could have become so estranged from her own children. At one point in their lives, they seemed inseparable, with the typical round of car pooling to school events and sports activities, meetings with teachers. Then there was an increasing bit of distance through high school as peers became so all-important, more separation during the college years, and now, well, now there is a call on the phone maybe once a week, if that often. They have moved from the daily intimacies to the weekly call, seemingly with less to talk about every week. They are still family, but at a distance.

The Greek word for "at a distance" is *makron*.[1] It is more common than we might think at first. After Jesus' arrest in the garden at Gethsemane, Matthew tells us that Peter followed "at a distance,"

71

until they reached the courtyard of the high priest. *Makron*. When Jesus was crucified, Matthew says that many women, having followed Jesus from Galilee, were also there, looking on from a distance. *Makron*.

From time to time we may find ourselves in a conversation circle with friends when someone starts to speak negatively about some person who is not present. Others join in. We may join in the gossip party ourselves, but even if we don't, though we know gossip is unchristian, we say nothing to stop the conversation. We don't want our friends to think that we are always the party's wet blanket, the person who can never let his hair down and just be a "regular person." So we follow Jesus, but at a distance. *Makron*.

Jesus once told the story of the prodigal son, and it is no secret that the figure of the father in that parable, with his forgiving love for his wayward son, is meant to represent God. So when the son returns to his father in the story, his father sees him "at a distance" — *makron* — and runs to him. His father makes up all the distance, all the *makron*, that stands between his errant son and the precious relationship he stands in need of reestablishing with his father. No wonder everyone loves this story. We *are* that son, we stand *makron* — at a distance — from God, and God had to take action to narrow the gap, to come closer to us.

This is what Peter was going on about when he preached in Jerusalem soon after the resurrection. Peter spoke to the crowd about Jesus, whom they had crucified, and told them who he really was. And when they wondered what they could do to be made right with this one who was the very anointed one of God, Peter told them: "Repent ... be baptized ... be forgiven ... receive the Holy Spirit ... for the promise is for you, for your children, and *for all who are far away* ..." at a distance. *Makron*.

So, if you feel sometimes as if you are at a distance from God, if there are those days when your prayers seem to bounce back at you off the ceiling, or you sometimes wonder if God cares or even if there is a God, much less whether you can be close to such a God, then the good news for us is this: we are the very people about whom Peter says these words. We are the ones at a distance, the very ones God had in mind when, in Christ, he came to us to save us.

Think for a moment who it is who was preaching this sermon to the crowd gathered in Jerusalem that day. It was Peter. Peter who had followed Jesus *at a distance* that day he was crucified, Peter who denied him three times before daybreak, Peter who had challenged his teacher not to go to Jerusalem and die, whom Jesus had called "Satan."

If anyone knew what it was to be at a distance from his Lord and Messiah, it was Peter. Yet the very first great sermon in the history of the Christian church came from his lips that day. He was far away, but Jesus' love brought him near again. He was at a distance, but God's love narrowed the gap. *Makron* turned to relationship because of the power of God.

It suggests to me that there is no distance from God at which we may find ourselves which cannot be more than made up by the effort to which God has gone for us in Christ.

The title of the sermon today takes its cue from verse 36 of the lesson: "Therefore let the entire house of Israel know with certainty that God has made him both Lord and Messiah, this Jesus whom you crucified." We may read this again and again and begin to think of Christ in three ways by means of this passage: he is Lord, he is Messiah, yet he is Crucified. In each, the question of our distance from God becomes a prominent issue.

To be Lord. This is an exalted Jesus, a divine Jesus, Jesus as seated at the right hand of God, Jesus as the second person of the Trinity. To be Lord is to be the one in power, the one in control. It is to be the owner of the manor, the one to whom everyone else on the property is to pay homage and tithe. It is the highest of the three titles for Jesus in this verse, from a human perspective; it comes first because if the others did, we might not recognize who *else* he is soon enough. Jesus is Lord. He is at one with the God who brought the slaves out of Egypt, who brought Israel across the sea, back from exile. It is this same Jesus whom John says was with God "in the beginning," and that without him nothing was made that was made. This is the highest view of Jesus, and if we were given only this view of him, we might despair of ever collapsing the distance between him and us. But it is only the first way the verse names him.

To be Messiah. This title for Jesus brings him closer. The word *Messiah* is a Hebrew word which is translated into Greek as *Christos*, and into English as "Christ." It means, simply, "anointed." There had been several messiahs in the Bible: Saul was one, David was one, Solomon was one. These were not gods but human beings who were chosen by God to serve both God and the people in a special way. They were anointed for their tasks, which set them apart in extraordinary ways, which is why they are so well-remembered all these centuries later. But for all the special nature of each of them, there is among them the reality that they are human, not divine. They are, in the end, people like us. Extraordinary, to be sure, but human. Jesus is Lord, but also Messiah; divine, yet anointed as a man to a human and earthly task.

To be Crucified. This is the title which brings the triple reality of the person of Jesus right into our own lives. It is this crucifixion which God uses to set aside the distance which had always separated us from God. The crucifixion of Jesus means that God knows in the most bitter and painful of ways what it is to be human and yet chooses even so to be in intimate relationship with humanity. God embraces us in the pain we know, because God has come to know pain through the passion of Jesus.

It is this triple reality about Jesus that empowers Peter, in the end, to say, "For the promise is for you, for your children, and for all who are far away, everyone whom the Lord our God calls to him."

If you feel distanced from God today, you are not unique, you are not odd, you are not out of step with the rest of humanity. You are, in fact, in the seat of blessing. You are the very one for whom God has gone to the trouble to be Lord, Messiah, and Crucified, to collapse the distance between you, to be in relationship with you and through you. It is for you. For you.

---

1. I am thankful for William Willimon's sermon "At A Distance," preached in the Duke University Chapel, April 14, 1996, and his background material on *makron* for this sermon.

All Things In Common
Are Not All Common Things

Now here is what I often think of as a passage of scripture with high potential for use as a brick-bat. At least it is often employed that way by folks who think the way the church moves ahead is by making people feel guilty and bad about things that are not their fault. Sometimes preachers read this and find it almost too tempting to stand before their congregations and extol the glories of the church in the New Testament version of the "good old days," so that everyone pretty much feels extra lousy that the good old days appear to be long-gone enough as to be well nigh unrecoverable. Yes, in the good old days — if only we could have lived then — why, folks in the church were just together, like a family, had all things in common, for crying out loud. Try suggesting that to a modern congregation, even one that claims to "preach the Bible." They had all things in common? What church practices that today, other than a few monastic orders, or loony cults? I'm already feeling like a faithless, no good so-and-so. This must be a really good sermon by that inappropriate-guilt measuring stick.

Before we descend into excessive guilt, though, we should probably read this and other scripture about the early church, remembering that whatever else we might feel justifiably guilty about in our lives, we ought not feel guilty for having been born into a century other than the first one. Not our fault. We should also probably recall the old tongue-in-cheek remark that nostalgia just isn't what it used to be. It never is.

This passage reminisces about those first days of the church's existence, when the fellowship shared everything, when wonders and signs were popping off the apostles' fingertips like firecrackers, when they spent time together in the Jerusalem Temple every day, when even their eating together was marked by words such as "glad," and "generous." There was goodwill even from those outside the church, and new members were flowing into the fellowship day by day. Yes, those were the days, weren't they? If only the church could simply have remained in those halcyon days.

But why didn't it? Why couldn't it? Why won't it? There are lots of reasons. If we were to read on in Acts beyond this idealized snapshot of the church's life in its first days, we would find that soon apostles will be winding up in jail for their preaching. Where at first those outside the fellowship had what Luke records as "the goodwill of all the people," that sentiment was not to last, not universally. Within a few years there would be persecution, imprisonment, even execution at the hands of those outside the fellowship. Even within the church, Ananias and Saphira would be found withholding funds from the fellowship, and lying about it to boot. Soon, Greek Christians and Hebrew Christians would be at odds over whether or not the church should continue all or even some of the Jewish synagogue and Temple practices. Even the apostles would disagree about this. Stephen would be murdered for his faith. Things looked really really golden in this passage, but the very faithfulness of the church would soon thrust it into a world that does not yet know nor yet value the witness of those whose lives have been given to Christ as Lord and Savior.

What we do have in this snapshot of the earliest life of the church is a memory picture, like our favorite memory of the way folks were customarily seated around the dinner table at the family Christmas dinner. Brother here, sister there, grandmother across the way, dad there, mom here. Now that mental picture is the stuff of Currier and Ives or of Norman Rockwell. But you and I know that underneath the idealized Ozzie and Harriet picture of such occasions, there has always lived the nitty-gritty day-to-day reality that just insists itself into the picture even on special days. The already-broken toy that lay in the living room and the tears that were still brimming on young eyelids about it; the fight you just had with your brother or sister over a chocolate bar; the angry glance that your mother shot at your father after some callous remark about the vegetables.

The purpose of golden memories is not to throw our ordinary lives into shadow, but to give us something to shoot for, an ideal about the way things can be in the kingdom. Just because we have things in common does not mean that all experience is common. Some of it is holy; sometimes we do not see how holy it is until we look back later, sometimes much later. Sometimes the ordinary stays ordinary in our memory for years, decades, until some present circumstance throws new light on it and it provides a vision of what could be from a totally unexpected place.

I have a friend who never thought what a good driving teacher his father was, for instance, until another two decades passed and he was the driving teacher whose didactic methods paled in comparison to his father's to the degree that both his daughters much preferred learning to drive with their mother in the passenger seat. That memory, now filled with nostalgia, of course, provided him with a tiny view of the way the world could be, perhaps even ought to be.

It is the golden moments of the church we need to recall when we hit the tough patches. They keep us going, keep us effective. A friend of mine serves a church in a community where a homeless woman froze to death one winter. His church remembered a time in their community when such a thing would have caused a paroxysm of self-examination in the community, and they set about with other churches to do something about it. The social service agencies said they could help but would need time — months — to get the paperwork and funding rolling. The churches said, that is fine, you keep talking about this and working out your procedures, but we are committed to an old vision where the church had all things in common, and we are going to go on without you. Join us when you can. And they did go on. They gave themselves to what they had in common, not to what distinguished them from one another.

We recall communities with schools where children could go and learn their lessons, and make faces at each other, and make eyes at one another, and cry and laugh, and no one ever worried about being shot to death in the school library. In a statistical summary for calendar year 1995, democratic nations were compared in regard to gun deaths of young people under 19. The results are astounding: in Japan there were none; in Great Britain, nineteen; in Germany, 59; in Canada, 153 — 231 total. In the United States, there were 5,285 — 260 in Texas alone!

In 1996 in New Zealand, Australia, Japan, Great Britain, Canada, and Germany — all countries with vigorously democratic governments and people who are as free as we are to go about their daily lives — the total number of gun murders for all those nations in 1996 was 377. This compares with 9,390 in the United States for the same year. The main difference between those countries and ours is that ownership of weapons is not considered a birthright of all citizens elsewhere as it is here. That, and the fact that perhaps the time has come for us to admit to ourselves that we have forgotten our more innocent times and become a nation perilously addicted to violence over a broad spectrum of human activity, from art, to cinema, to recreation, to domestic relations.

I don't know about you, but even though the reality is different today following the gruesome and senseless violence of recent years in our public schools, I do not want to let go of that golden memory of violence-free schools and violence-free homes as a source of thinking about how things should be in our culture. We all can remember a day when no one would ever have thought to suggest laws permitting ordinary citizens to carry concealed weapons around in public, when a person who enjoyed hunting would never have thought to go out looking for semi-automatic weapons or stockpiling the makings of bombs in the basement. I have a friend whose Scottish cousin, living in Great Britain, a country with some of the tightest gun control laws and enforcement in the world, expresses utter amazement at the gun culture of the United States. While people in Britain, on the whole, do not own guns, they are not enslaved, they do not find themselves living under a dictator. They also do not shoot their family members with anything approaching the regularity we do here. A magazine ad ran recently, picturing the barrel of a handgun pointed directly at the reader, saying ominously, "The person most likely to kill you with a gun already has a key to your house." Other vigorously democratic and free countries do not witness school children blasting away at each other with weapons that would be the envy of many third world militias, and yet they remain free. What can we learn from their golden dream?

The annual General Assembly of the Presbyterian Church (U.S.A.) two years ago passed a resolution calling upon all Presbyterians to work toward removing handguns and assault weapons from our homes and communities, adding that church members should develop community strategies and create sanctuaries of safety for our children. If our commitment to the commonweal, our commitment to the common good, can recall a time in our lives together when we first took into account what was best for the most, and only secondarily what is most profitable for the individual, we might find in that a vision for a kind of world we would like to see again. We might even get motivated to say to those who make the laws and enforce them that the time for tolerance of the American gun culture as well as the culture of violence has come to an end, that we have an older and better vision, one which values the good of the whole over the presumed individual rights of those who cling to means of violence.

To be the church sometimes means simply to be the fellowship, that, holding our vision in common, cries out "Enough!" as did Rosa Parks one day on a bus in Montgomery, Alabama; as did John Witherspoon when he became the only clergyman to sign the Declaration of Independence; as did Francis of Assisi when he left behind the war-loving feudal life he had known to work with the poor; as did Abraham Lincoln when he put pen to paper to set the slaves free at last; as did Lyndon Johnson when he introduced legislation to put an end to racial discrimination at the polls; as did Martin Luther, when he helped put an end to the selling of the church's birthright of the grace of Christ.

79

When in the church we have all things in common, it turns out that they are anything but all common things. They become holy things, a holy calling. We need to pray about our calling whenever we experience dramatic events in our nation; we need to pray earnestly about the calling of our church community as we confront the issues of the day.

Covering Our Ears And Shouting

In the earliest experience of the church, the apostles soon discovered that their teaching and preaching duties were taking an incredible amount of energy. As the community of believers grew in numbers, and they continued in their commitment to hold all things in common, it became obvious that some details of the life of the community would need more attention than the twelve apostles themselves could give. It was decided to appoint deacons to serve the needs of the church, particularly the needs of the poor and widows who could no longer care for themselves. Seven were appointed. These folks were the first deacons, and one of them was a man named Stephen.

Stephen's career was shortened because of his determination to be more than a silent servant of the poor. In the midst of his work he could not contain his enthusiasm for the gospel, and he did all he could to spread the word about Jesus — the one who got the church interested in the poor to begin with. He spoke about it so much and so often, that it wasn't long before the local religious authorities called him in for a chat about his views. In their opinion, he was doing damage to their historic faith. But they didn't bother to ask him; they called in false witnesses who would say anything in front of a courtroom in order to stay out of trouble with the law themselves.

Even so, when Stephen was provided an opportunity to defend himself, he delivered one of the longest speeches in the Bible, an eloquent review of the history of Israel and the saving acts of

God throughout that history. It was so long, in fact, that one commentator joked that he wondered why they didn't kill him sooner. At the conclusion of his speech, Acts reports that his judges:

> *When they heard these things, they became enraged and ground their teeth at Stephen. But filled with the Holy Spirit, he gazed into heaven and saw the glory of God and Jesus standing at the right hand of God. "Look," he said, "I see the heavens opened and the Son of Man standing at the right hand of God!" But they covered their ears, and with a loud shout all rushed together against him. Then they dragged him out of the city and began to stone him; and the witnesses laid their coats at the feet of a young man named Saul. While they were stoning Stephen, he prayed, "Lord Jesus, receive my spirit." Then he knelt down and cried out in a loud voice, "Lord, do not hold this sin against them." When he had said this, he died.*

Verse 57 stands out in my mind for some reason. It is so human, so much the way we can be when we are so steeped in our errors and our prejudices that we cannot bear to hear a word of truth: "But they covered their ears, and with a loud shout all rushed together against him." It was, I think, the last straw. They could not bear to hear any more. Of course, their very actions that followed fully demonstrated the accuracy of what Stephen had said: that they were a stiff-necked people whose ears and hearts had not been committed to the Lord from day one, and that they were forever opposing the Holy Spirit. He was dead right. *Dead* right. And that is just what they set about doing, of course, opposing the Holy Spirit with stoppered ears and hearts hardened to the consistency of granite.

I have a friend who shared a vivid parental memory of a feature of traveling as a family with young children. It usually occurred late in the day, after a long day of travel. One child reaches across the seat to touch the other; the other reciprocates. Accusations are hurled back and forth over who did what to whom first, and soon, the intervention of the cavalry is requested in the form of mom or dad.

One feature of this experience stays in my mind. It is when one child tries to tell the other something he isn't supposed to do, and the other puts hands over both ears, blocking out all sound from her sibling by intoning the famous melody known to children the world over, with the following lyrics: "I'm not listening, I'm not listening, nyah, nyah, nyah, nyah, nyaaah, nyah." It's an interesting tune, that little one. It seems to be universally known as a taunting tune, three tones, always used in the same fashion, sometimes followed by tongues stuck out, sometimes not, there are multiple variations on the theme as well as particular performance styles. But the outcome is always the very same: someone is not listening and stoppering her ears deliberately to avoid doing so.

Now that is what I call a more or less belligerent method for avoiding having to hear what someone else has to say. It is an effective, if childish, way of saying the conversation is over; whatever you have to say, I'm not interested, you are wasting your breath, this discussion is closed. It is exactly what those who charged at Stephen did. Did you notice it as the scripture was read? "But they covered their ears" and ran at Stephen with "a loud shout," it says. Maybe it was an ancient version of "nyah, nyah, nyah, nyah, nyaaah, nyah" that they shouted. What does it take to "unstopper" childish, unlistening ears, I wonder?

There are so many surprising things about this little passage. There are many similarities in the death of Stephen, of course, to the death of Jesus: they were both tried before what amounted to religious kangaroo courts; as Jesus died on the cross and as Stephen died under a hail of stones, both cried out to their Lord to receive their spirits, and both asked for forgiveness for those who were literally in the act of killing them. And the deaths, while not an act of God, both caused the spread rather than the end of the gospel. Here is another parallel. It wasn't some high Jewish official who died for the sins of the people, but a carpenter's son from Nazareth. Likewise, it was not an apostle or high church official who became the first Christian martyr, but a previously unknown table-serving deacon. Servants, both of them.[1]

83

There was another servant on the scene that day, holding the coats of those who were doing the difficult, dirty work of stoning a human being to death in the hot sun, not an easy or quick sort of execution. In the end of the passage, there is that little insight into the one who, one day soon, would become Paul the apostle. Here he is still known by his Hebrew name, Saul. And here, of course, he fully approved of the goings-on that had been going on. It most certainly never occurred to him at that moment, as Stephen shed his precious blood for the faith he loved more than his own life, becoming the first martyr for his faith, that in a few years time this Saul-turned-Paul would be another martyr, just as seventeen-year-old Cassie Bernall became when she fell in the school library in Littleton, Colorado, from a shot that came when she said to her killer that, yes, she believed in God. She died next to her Bible, it is said, her short life closed out for her while thoughts of her love for God were in her mind. She would not relinquish her faith. Students who were nearby said she paused for a moment before answering whether she believed in God, as if she were counting the potential cost. Then she made her witness, as did Paul, as did Stephen, bravely, unflinchingly.

Now, what do these stories about Stephen, about Paul, about Cassie Bernall have to say to people who are not likely to come near martyrdom, which is most of us? Elie Wiesel is a writer and philosopher/theologian who survived Hitler's death camps and reflected after the Columbine High School massacre, that it was so unnerving that Hitler is *still* killing people. He once said that suffering always has two parts: the act itself and our response to it. Stephen set a Christlike standard in his response to his suffering as stones rained down on him, saying, "Lord, do not hold this sin against them."

In Littleton, and other tense situations where violence has torn the fabric of the community, anonymous death threats have been received by families of the perpetrators. That, of course, is one response that could be chosen, and who could fail to see why some would resort to it? Yet it abandons allegiance with what is good to join with the enemy we thought we were fighting. Whatever else we may think, we are not permitted to follow such behavior in the name of Christ, who forgave his tormentors from his cross, and whose followers have showered blessings on the world that once cursed them.

So if Wiesel is right, that suffering has two parts, the first of which is generally out of the hands of the sufferer, what are we to do, in Christ's name, about the second? What is to be our response?

If we had chosen to be at home instead of in this sanctuary today, we could probably have turned on one of several religious broadcasts and received the totally-happy Christian message that if we will support this or that television ministry, we will receive healing and blessing and happiness all our days. But, of course, it is a lie, or at least not the complete truth. The difficult but good news that Stephen and Paul experienced is that there is something in the world worth dying for, something of such value that it is also worth living for. They seem to have known it when they saw it.[2]

Not everyone is called to be a martyr in this way, of course. In fact, in our lifetimes, few are. But all still need to consider the second half of Elie Wiesel's equation, the need to respond to suffering in some way. Our response, for most of us on this non-martyred side of the equation, will be to work to alleviate suffering while refusing to hate those who cause it. That is a tough task for a believer, a well nigh impossible one for an unbeliever. But the examples of Jesus and Stephen make this the only legitimate Christian response: "Father, forgive them ..."

Father, forgive. It is such a difficult demand on believers, and yet it stands before us, insistently. Forgive, forgive, forgive. Perhaps Frederick Buechner deserves to have a last word, a word which opens our ears and stops our incommunicative shouting. He said, "When somebody you've wronged forgives you, you're spared the dull and self-diminishing throb of a guilty conscience. When you forgive somebody who has wronged you, you're spared the dismal corrosion of bitterness and wounded pride. For both parties, forgiveness means the freedom again to be at peace inside their own skins ..."[3]

Jesus said, "Peace I leave with you." That was his response to a world that would cause him intense suffering. How can we make our aim anything less?

1. Eugene Lowry, "Stones And Bones," *Best Sermons 7*, James Cox, ed. (Harper Collins, 1994), p. 191.

2. *Ibid.*, p. 192.

3. Frederick Buechner, *Wishful Thinking* (Harper & Row, 1973), p. 29.

How To Be Christian
Without Being Religious

One thing about ancient Athens. It was a marketplace for new ideas. In verse 21 of this chapter of Acts, Luke tells us that everyone who lived in Athens liked to spend time telling and hearing the latest new thing.

Greece itself was a cradle for numerous philosophical and religious movements, and combinations of the two, where philosophy became religion and religion became philosophy. And Athens was a center for religious inquiry. If a modern day actor can make a name for himself in New York, then chances are good his career will be successful anywhere. Similarly, if a wandering preacher of any religion of the first century could gain a hearing in Athens, chances were good that his star was on the rise.

So Paul spoke up in Athens. The occasion was unusual in itself. He never intended to preach in Athens, really. He just happened to be there waiting to meet up with Silas and Timothy so they could continue their missionary journeys together. As he waited, he went walking through the bustling city, and couldn't help noticing the incredible number and variety of religious shrines, temples, and trinkets that were in evidence throughout the region.

He looked at these things, not with the eyes of a modern person. When we see statues of the Greek gods, and amulets worn by people of the first century, we are inclined to look at them as works of art. Not too many people are serious followers of Zeus or Diana today, although, anything is possible. But when Paul saw them, there were thousands who saw the same things we see as art, yet who saw them through religious eyes. These temples, shrines and trinkets were as precious to them as our Bibles are to us today. Paul saw them through the eyes of a trained rabbi as well as a Christian believer. The Jews could never countenance the worship of man-made objects, but they never worried too much if others did.

Now Paul was in a predicament. He knew that because of Christ, Greeks as well as Jews were to be the chosen people of God. These children of God were worshiping idols of stone and silver, and he couldn't remain silent. He spoke up. And for his troubles, he was summoned to stand before the city council and defend his teaching. Rather like medical practitioners today, in the roiling religious atmosphere of Athens not just anyone could hang out a shingle and begin speaking of things religious. The city fathers wanted to know more about this strange doctrine of which Paul spoke.

The passage for today contains Luke's summary of the sermon that Paul delivered that day.

Paul began by saying that he saw in Athens evidence that the people of that city were very religious. I don't know about you, but I'm accustomed to hearing such a comment from another person as a compliment. On the occasion of a funeral service, pastors will often hear a family member say that Uncle Henry was a very religious man. And we know that in every way they mean that to be taken as a positive remark. It is meant as a compliment. But could Paul have meant it in that way? Is there something he can teach us if we are people inclined to call ourselves religious?

The Athenians were thoroughly pagan. They did not have the slightest notion who Jesus was, and if they knew about the Jews, they certainly gave little indication that they had been affected by Jewish belief or practice: the abundance of temples and statuary would have been ample evidence of that. Yet Paul called them "in every way very religious."

What do you suppose he was trying to say? Scurrying to a Bible dictionary can be a revealing exercise. Much as we may be inclined to call ourselves religious people, the Bible doesn't think much of the word, and uses the term that Paul used here only once. It is *desidemon*. It means, literally, "fear of the demons or of the supernatural." What Paul was saying was that the people of Athens were highly superstitious! Rarely are pastors told by a mourner at a funeral that Uncle Henry was a very superstitious man ... not if they want to compliment Uncle Henry!

We have to ask ourselves what Paul had in mind, using such a comment to open his speech. Did he want to say that because the people of Athens were very religious, they were going to be able to understand God's plan of salvation for them, as we might have suspected on first reading? Or was he saying the surprising thing, that *in spite of their very religious — superstitious — nature*, in spite of their inclination to put too much weight on the ritual and the magical in their religious behavior, in spite of all that, *God can make his plan of salvation available to them anyway*?

Paul was simply stating a fact, not a compliment. Their minds were clouded with unnecessary fears. Even so, God could speak to them in Jesus Christ. If we know any truly superstitious people, we know what kind of thing Paul had seen. People can be controlled by unnatural fears of cats crossing their paths, going out a different door than the one by which they entered a house, avoiding ladders overhead. Paul says, in the 25th verse, "Nor does [God] need anything that we can supply by working for him, since it is he himself who gives life and breath and everything else to everyone."

What a view of the world! It is not a place to be endured, feared, and tolerated. Rather, it is an evidence of God's good nature, which is to bestow gifts upon humanity, as a father bestows gifts on his children.

In our thinking about evangelism, which pastors and church committees are consistently encouraging us to do, we can find an answer to another question in this sermon delivered by Paul to the people of Athens. If ever we have said to ourselves, "I'd like to tell other people about my faith, but I wouldn't know what to say," we ought to take the cue from Paul. He provides a good example of a way in which any believer can share the Good News without requiring that the other people in the conversation be biblical experts beforehand.

Who did Paul quote to them when he said to them that God is not far from any of us? Did he quote the Old Testament prophets or Moses? No. When he said, "In him we live and move and have our being," he was quoting Epimenides, a pagan Greek poet from Crete. And when he said, "We too are his children," he was quoting the pagan Cilician poet Aratus. I think there is a very important lesson here for us, for anyone who undertakes the basic Christian responsibility of telling another about the Good News of Jesus Christ. Paul began with the people, quoting from their own poets, reaching out to them, where they were, with words they would understand. He did not begin where he might have preferred them to be.

It's easy to preach to people who are thoroughly familiar with the Bible. I have an easy job, preaching to you, the committed and faithful ones. It is you who have the more demanding job of evangelism, for you are called to tell the Good News to a world that in many ways hasn't the slightest idea what you are talking about, that sells its goods by appealing to the lowest instincts of all of us. If you don't think we preach the gospel in a strange land, then turn on the television for a short time and count the number of minutes that pass before you encounter a Christian theme ... unless you are on a religious channel ... perhaps even then.

Paul approached those Athenians the same way that God approaches us in the person of Jesus. God didn't wait for us to become experts in biblical literature. Pastors and youth leaders have the privilege in ministry of seeing young people begin to look at Jesus through eyes of faith, and they would be the first to tell us that they did not wait until they were Bible experts before they made a commitment to follow him. God has simply said in Jesus Christ that salvation is available to everyone *now*. There is no residency requirement. No amount of religious hoopla can purchase it for us. It is purchased already. It is ours now, in just the shape we are in at this very moment. In a way, the church should be a "come as you are" party. Paul spoke to those Athenians through the poets they knew and understood, using that as a means to introduce them to Jesus. We can do the same.

Everyone we meet has at some time asked a religious question, just like those Athenians: "Why is there death? Is there a God who cares? What must I do to have a happy life?" All these are religious questions. All of them provide an entrée to superstition, or a word of Christian Good News. We can lay hold of that, just as Paul did, without feeling it necessary to do a lot of fancy quoting from all the minor prophets in the Bible.

I'd like to close by asking two questions today. 1) What does membership in the church mean in light of what Paul is saying? 2) What can someone who cannot yet call himself a believer still learn from Paul's words?

First, what does membership in the church mean in light of Paul's sermon in Athens? *It means a commitment to take the Good News to the nations.* Out of these doors and into the streets. No matter how unlikely the receiver of this word of Good News might appear to us to be, if we are willing to speak with him rather than to him, willing to meet him where he is, rather than require him to sit in a pew for a few weeks before we will go to the trouble to speak to him, then we will be true members of the church of Jesus Christ. This is not a club we have here, but a fellowship that reaches out in love. That outreach must go on continually, or we are no people of God. We must take the Word to others, and we must share it in ways they can understand.

Second, if there are people here asking what Christian commitment means, who are ready to ask, but not yet ready to commit themselves to the Lordship of Jesus Christ, what does Paul have to say to you? A great deal. In reality, Paul's sermon is intended more for you than for believers. He would want us to know that *we need not be religious in order to earn God's love.* God's love has already been expressed exquisitely. His love is primary. Our decision whether or not to accept that love is secondary. We can love him because he first loved us. As the Greek poet said, "We too are his children." He has told us in the man Jesus Christ that he loves us in this very moment, in this very situation, whether happy or sad, well-adjusted or confused. In each and every circumstance which people in the real world can find themselves, God's love waits to reach out and heal, and redeem, and challenge, and call forth.

What does it take for us to call ourselves Christian? Certainly not that we go to great lengths to prove to others that we are religious. Merely that we accept the gift that has already been given, the love of God in Jesus Christ, the man that God raised up from death to give life to the world.

Looking Up, Looking Out

Alan Paton was a courageous South African author whose courage was manifest in his novels, written during the vicious apartheid era in his country. He wrote historical novels about his homeland, courageous novels which spoke more of truth than of fiction. In his book, *Ah, But Your Land Is Beautiful* (Scribners, 1981), he described a meeting between the white headmaster of a school, Mr. Mansfield, and a black man, Mr. Nene, who was a government civil servant. Mr. Nene's job was to deliver messages from the South African courts to the unlucky black people who had managed to cross up the numerous and punitive South African apartheid laws.

Mr. Mansfield decided to resign his position because the government would not allow him to continue sports matches between his white school and a neighboring black school. He resigned because his personal limit had finally been reached, and he had determined that the government was asking too much of him, making demands upon the black population that he could no longer tolerate or overlook. As the black messenger of the court, Mr. Nene came to Mr. Mansfield's office, Mansfield was worried. Had he come to deliver a summons that Mansfield was to appear in court?

His fears were soon relieved. Mr. Nene, it turns out, only wanted to see him. He had never seen a white man willing to give up a prestigious position on behalf of black Africans before. He simply wanted to see him, to speak with him briefly, because, as it turns out, Mr. Nene had decided to resign his position too, and with much more to lose than Mansfield. He wanted to resign, he

93

said, because if a white man can show his courage in such a way, how could a black man continue as a servant of such an evil system? Nene had determined that he, too, must resign.

Nene added, "I am going to get wounded ... not only by the government, but by my own people as well ... Some will say, 'Why don't you stay with your own people? ... Why get mixed up with white people, who are rich while you are poor?' ... I don't worry about the wounds. When I go up there, which is my intention, the Big Judge will say to me, 'Where are your wounds?' And if I say I haven't any, he will say, 'Was there nothing to fight for?' I couldn't stand that question."

Mr. Nene, whether he knew it or not, had a very biblical understanding of the meaning of the Ascension. He had seen not only the promise of his faith for the future, but the fact that the promise, if really to be believed, must shape the present, must make us into different people than we have ever been before.

The Ascension scene, as it was described in the reading from Acts, is particularly mystifying in our scientific age, an age which prides itself on asking factual questions and expecting factual answers. The picture of a man, once dead, now appearing to his disciples, now disappearing, and ultimately disappearing into the clouds — this is almost more than we can take in. Some solve the problem by saying that God did it and that is that. But that is to accept a solution that is too small, robbing us of a richer, fuller understanding of what Luke meant by describing the scene just the way he did.

Our closest parallel to the image of Christ disappearing behind a cloud is probably the televised pictures of the space shuttles, as they are thrown into orbit on the backs of tremendous, roaring rocket engines. But this scene from Acts is nothing like that. Are we to believe the picture that one literalist painted, that the last view the disciples had of Jesus was of the bottoms of his feet as he rose in the air above their heads?

In truth, the scene of the Ascension is a materially inadequate way of describing a spiritual reality. The favored kings of Israel all ascended the throne with great fanfare. Much to-do was made over such ascensions; some of our psalms have been created for just such occasions. There grew up in Israel the belief that anyone chosen of God would ascend to him. The traditions in the Bible tell us that Moses was taken up this way, as were Elijah, Ezra, and Abraham. The ascension was seen by Bible writers as further indication that Jesus was the chosen one of God. It in no way seemed as fantastic to them as it does to us.

Luke says that "a cloud took him out of their sight." This was not a simple cumulonimbus. Recall that the Israelites in the desert followed a "pillar of cloud" during their exodus sojourn, that Peter and the other two saw Jesus in a cloud during his transfiguration, that in the Bible, a cloud represented in this way suggests the presence of God. Jesus was received into God's presence right before their eyes. How would *you* have put that into words? It seems to me that the account in Acts is not so fantastic when we see it that way. It is a way of describing the great affirmation that Jesus was received by the God who loved him, that when our children ask us "Where is Jesus now?" we can answer with the disciples that he lives smack in the center of God's love. Right in the very center.

In the old Latin Mass for Ascension day, the choir sang "Deus Ascendit": "God has gone up." Does this mean that God in Christ has gone up, away from the secular world, abandoned us to our own sorry devices? No, William Willimon once observed that the choir does not sing "Deus abscondit" — "God has absconded, deserted." They sing "Deus ascendit," "God has ascended," has begun in heaven what is yet to be accomplished on earth. Christ is gone up, not to forsake us, but to continue to redeem us.

As the shadow of Nazism darkened Europe, Karl Barth, the great modern Reformed theologian, said he rediscovered the necessity of the Ascension. When lights go out, it's always good to remember who is in charge.

This is the physical reminder that no matter how things may look, Jesus has taken up authority over the world of which he is Lord. As Mr. Nene would have said, the "Big Judge is on his throne," the world doesn't really belong to the violent, the power grabbers, the ones who quote scripture in order to justifying stealing what belongs to others. The disciples, for whatever reason, were convinced that Jesus was at the very center of things, and this sent them back into Jerusalem with shouts of joy and celebration.

The angels that sent them on their way stopped them from doing what we so often want to do, stopped them from looking up when they really needed to look out. It was time to stop gazing into heaven and start looking for evidence of his rule on earth. Because no matter who is in the White House or what the newspapers say, human authorities are not in charge. Christ is ascended to rule.

Anyone can see that God's reign is not fully established, that we are not living under God's rule in the world as we know it. To think so is tantamount to keeping our heads in the clouds, looking skyward in hopes of one more view of Jesus, stopping our ears to the admonitions of the angel to get about the work ahead of us in Jerusalem and the world. Looking up in order not to have to see suffering humanity around us, war and threat of war, this is a heresy that our passage from Acts would have us reject.

The disciples, in danger of getting cricks in their necks from their cloud-gazing, were reminded by the angelic visitation that their task was not to scan the skies for signs of Jesus. Their task was to get off that mountain and be about the work that Jesus had only begun. In the old *Revised Standard Version* translation of the opening of this passage, following the 24 chapters of his Gospel account, Luke declares, "In the first book, Theophilus, I wrote about all that Jesus had begun to do and to teach ..." The work of Jesus was only just begun when he was taken up into that cloud, his kingdom just under way. His work was to continue in the lives and work of these people he left standing on the mountaintop. It is a work which remains to be completed. We are the next generation of cloud-gazers in the line of the disciples.

More than a few commentators have suggested that this book's common name should be changed from the "Acts of the Apostles" to the "Acts of the Holy Spirit," since the book recounts the continuing work of Jesus through his Spirit-empowered church.

The task for these followers was no longer to look up for Jesus, but to look outward for him. It is the continuing task of those who follow Jesus to look out for the dispossessed, the hungry, the wounded, the spiritually dead and dying, all in a world with material plenty but a poverty of compassion. It is the task of the outward-looking church to utter the difficult word of judgment upon a world so fond of short-term advantage, so lacking in long-term life.

Looking out among the faces of those around us, we begin to see his face again. When Jesus said, "You shall be my witnesses," it was not a command, but a promise to be trusted. Where Jesus' disciples go, his witness lives in them. That is his promise. Where there is something, as Mr. Nene said, worth fighting for, we have his promise that we will not be abandoned. It is a promise that comes another step toward us at Pentecost, when the Spirit was unleashed on those who were willing to look outward.

Even in these lazy late-spring afternoons, as we move between graduation and work, in what is left of the spring, looking forward to the days of summer when life can drift a bit more slowly, even in these days when the driving purpose behind work or school or vacuuming the carpet for the one thousandth time seems obscure, even now it is important to remember who rules, who it is that sends us out with the promise that we will be his witnesses.

Restoring The Future

Do you know what Ascension Day is? In many Christian traditions, that day is a festival as important as Good Friday or Thanksgiving. It is a day which comes exactly forty days after Easter. It is the commemoration of Jesus' assumption into heaven which was the subject of our reading from Acts today. It marks the conclusion of his resurrection appearances and the opening of the ministry of the Holy Spirit through the work of the church.

While Ascension Day isn't a big holiday in the U.S.A., I know of a pastor in South Africa who says it is a significant cultural celebration there, as it is in many other countries. All the schools are let out for the day, many people go for a picnic or a family outing, much as happens on our Memorial Day. I just hope as many go to church to hear what the word Ascension refers to!

Still, some faith communities here in the U.S.A. do make a bit of a fuss over Ascension Day. There is a Lutheran church in Missouri where a handful of people show up at the church a couple of hours before their Thursday evening Ascension Day service each year and begin filling up helium balloons.[1] Hundreds of balloons are filled into a large white bag made up of several bed sheets, sewn together. The man-made "cloud" is then pinned at the end and released to float about over the heads of the worshipers like a prize blimp at a professional basketball arena.

The pastor of the church says the sight is glorious in its own way, but also befuddling to visitors. The "cloud" has been known to dive bomb the candelabra, and so it sometimes has to be tethered with fish line. He says the "net effect of this soaring cloud routine is the 'crooked neck syndrome.' ... Preaching in this setting is a challenge because worshipers rarely bother to look at the pulpit. But that upwards obsession is what Ascension Day is all about."[2] One of the oldest tricks in the book for mischief-minded big-city kids is to stand on a street corner craning necks back to look at some non-existent phenomenon in the sky, just to see how many people you can influence to follow your gaze upwards. The temptation is almost irresistible to those of us who are suggestible anyway. I recall a Baptist preacher who once preached a Sunday evening service, eyes fixed on the back of the church ceiling, shouting, "Can you see Jesus coming now, in his GLO-ry?" It was all the worshipers could do to resist turning in their seats to see if the bricks on the back wall were about to give way to the returning Savior.

I have a friend who remembers being dropped off by his parents for his freshman year at college. Just days before he had gotten himself all packed up, ready to head for school, and asked his older brother if he thought he looked like a college man. "No," he said, "you look like a freshman." A couple of days later, he knew his brother was right. He was standing there in his ridiculous freshman beanie — shows you how old this friend is — on the driveway into his new school, in a new city, in a new state, where he knew hardly anyone. He waved at his parents as they drove away, waving back at him. He continued watching as they disappeared into the distance, over the hill, off into a cloud of mystery as it were, their day-to-day lives now officially separated from his. An old chapter of his life was now behind him, a new one was opening. Bright as his future was going to be, it didn't feel all that bright at that moment. And all the previous conversations about his future, about the school work that lay ahead of him, all the dinner table speculations about the universe of possibilities that waited over the horizon seemed pretty small compensation just then for the certainties and securities of the life of a child and teenager in a loving home that he had known up to that moment.

I imagine that in a much more significant way, the disciples had similar feelings as they watched Jesus being swallowed up in the heavenly cloud, removed from them so that he had officially become, now, a memory, not a presence anymore. Oh sure, he had promised them a new sense of his presence through the Holy Spirit, but they had some in-the-meantime to get through before the Spirit came to them, and in the meantime their future without Jesus' physical presence didn't look anywhere nearly as promising as their past had been when they used to join him by the lakeside.

They stood there, eyes straining to see the last glimpse of him, realizing that they were now a people of the past, who must plod through the present without much of a future. How could their future be restored when their whole attention could only focus on the past and the One now absent?

Many of the rising generations go through such periods of hopelessness. The certainties of childhood give way to the confusion and dislocation of adolescence and young adulthood. The unquestioned love of parents is replaced by the fickle, inconstant affections of peers, the material and philosophical securities of trusting children turn easily into the futureless cynicisms of those who discover they can take nothing in their adult world for granted. How to restore a future when only the past seems secure and what lies ahead looms with threatening uncertainties?

The disciples, while not adolescent, nonetheless had similar feelings of dislocation. They asked one of the oldest and most deeply religious questions in the world: "What now?" It is a two-word question that is not only curious about the future, but wonders if there will even be a future. What now? Now that we are all grown up, what now? Think of the times in life when this is one of the most appropriate questions to be asked: I've graduated from high school or college; what now? I'm married; what now? I'm baptized; what now? I'm hired; what now? I've built my dream home; what now? I've retired; what now? I've joined the church; what now?

When we rebel, when we are angry, when we are depressed — perhaps especially when we are depressed — it is so often because we see no future, because we ask the age-old question, "What now?" and we cannot find our way to an answer.

Naturally enough, the disciples' question of Jesus before he went off into orbit had to do with restoration. "Lord, is this the time when you will restore the kingdom to Israel?" Lord, can't we go back? Lord, we miss the good old days, will you bring them back? Politicians have won elections for centuries by promising to do just that, but it is a mirage, a trick done with mirrors, for what was can never be again. Life moves forward even when we look backward — or upward. They wanted what we often want when we undertake painstaking restoration of old buildings or automobiles: a piece of the past. When finished, though, the past does not reemerge. We still live in the present, awaiting a word to move us into a hope-filled future.

Even more difficult than restoring pieces of the past would be the building of a twenty-second century car or building. How would we know if we'd gotten it right? "Ahead of his time" is a phrase invariably preceded by a past-tense verb: "He was ahead of his time." We only see it in retrospect, looking back. The future remains a mystery. The past seems at least safe, while the future appears to be impossibly distant, unknowable. Lord, won't you just restore the kingdom? That we could understand. We know what the old kingdom looked like. But Jesus just made this promise: "You will receive power when the Holy Spirit comes ... You will become my witnesses."

So there they stood, gazing off into the cloud, wondering, "What now?" Then along came two men in white to ask them a question which Will Rogers may well have been paraphrasing when he once said, "Even if you're on the right track, you'll get run over if you just sit there." Jesus' prayer in John 17 entrusted the disciples' future to God. Now the disciples must move toward that future. But how?

Well, they began in the order that Jesus had told them, one step at a time. First, back to Jerusalem; then they would be called into the rest of the nation, even to Samaria, even to the whole world. That's where their work stands today. Imagine! There they stood in their freshman beanies, being told the future was promise-filled, the world would be their pulpit. All that was needed to grasp it was to take one step at a time, place one foot in front of the other in the way he told them to go. They returned to Jerusalem, and there we see the little church beginning to take shape, with the disciples, some unnamed women, Jesus' mother, Mary, and Jesus' brothers. Followers, friends, family, just like the make-up of most churches today. They took the first step toward the future, and soon they would receive the power which Jesus had promised.

The same is true for us. Take one step toward Christ in faith, and he will run toward us the rest of the way. Our future in him is bright. Just go there. Just trust him.

---

1. Peter W. Marty, "Up, Up, And Away," in *Christian Century*, May 15, 1996, p. 543.

2. *Ibid.*

Books In This Cycle A Series

GOSPEL SET
It's News To Me! Messages Of Hope For Those Who Haven't Heard
Sermons For Advent/Christmas/Epiphany
Linda Schiphorst McCoy

Tears Of Sadness, Tears Of Gladness
Sermons For Lent/Easter
Albert G. Butzer, III

Pentecost Fire: Preaching Community In Seasons Of Change
Sermons For Sundays After Pentecost (First Third)
Schuyler Rhodes

Questions Of Faith
Sermons For Sundays After Pentecost (Middle Third)
Marilyn Saure Breckenridge

The Home Stretch: Matthew's Vision Of Servanthood In The End-Time
Sermons For Sundays After Pentecost (Last Third)
Mary Sue Dehmlow Dreier

FIRST LESSON SET
Long Time Coming!
Sermons For Advent/Christmas/Epiphany
Stephen M. Crotts

Restoring The Future
Sermons For Lent/Easter
Robert J. Elder

Formed By A Dream
Sermons For Sundays After Pentecost (First Third)
Kristin Borsgard Wee

Living On One Day's Rations
Sermons For Sundays After Pentecost (Middle Third)
Douglas B. Bailey

Let's Get Committed
Sermons For Sundays After Pentecost (Last Third)
Derl G. Keefer

SECOND LESSON SET
Holy E-Mail
Sermons For Advent/Christmas/Epiphany
Dallas A. Brauninger

Access To High Hope
Sermons For Lent/Easter
Harry N. Huxhold

Acting On The Absurd
Sermons For Sundays After Pentecost (First Third)
Gary L. Carver

A Call To Love
Sermons For Sundays After Pentecost (Middle Third)
Tom M. Garrison

Distinctively Different
Sermons For Sundays After Pentecost (Last Third)
Gary L. Carver